Victims of Piracy

Victims of Piracy

The Admiralty Court
1575 – 1678

Evelyn Berckman

Hamish Hamilton: *London*

First published in Great Britain 1979
by Hamish Hamilton Ltd
Garden House, 57–59 Long Acre, London WC2E 9JL

Copyright © 1979 by Evelyn Berckman

British Library Cataloguing in Publication Data

Berckman, Evelyn
  Victims of piracy.
  1. Great Britain—History—Elizabeth,
  1568–1603—Sources 2. Great Britain—
  History—Stuarts, 1603–1714—Sources
  3. Pirates—England
  364.1'35   DA350

  ISBN 0–241–10105–0

Printed in Great Britain by
Western Printing Services, Bristol

In memory
of
S. L. Drummond-Jackson
a conqueror of pain and of
fear of pain, equally

Contents

PART I

I   Introduction   3

II   The Admiralty Court   5

III   Straight Piracies   15

IV   Piracy and Murder   36

V   Suspensus erat   41

VI   Buggery   51

VII   Peine Forte et Dure   53

VIII   A Horror Story   56

PART II

IX   An Atrocity   63

X   The Smooth Talker and the Dupe   68

XI   Perils of the Sea   76

XII   Two-Faced John Exton   83

XIII   A Bungler   90

XIV   The Charge of Cowardice   93

XV   Local Voices   99

XVI   A Mystery   105

XVII   Allsorts   108

XVIII   Letters of Reprisal   113

XIX   The Gap   118

XX   Presente: The Kinges Most Excelente Majestie   120

XXI   Obstacles and Clearway   126

Index   129

Illustrations

Between pages 22 and 23

1 SYMBOLS OF THE ADMIRALTY COURT
   a Seal
   By kindness of the Public Record Office
   b The Oar
   By kindness of the Lord Chancellor, the Lord Chief Justice
   and Trustees of the Exhibition of Legal Costumes, Law
   Courts
   c Modern Seal,
   By kindness of Mr Ricks, Admiralty Marshal, Law Courts

2 Indictment, Peine Forte et Dure
   By kindness of the Public Record Office

3 Warrant, Peine Forte et Dure
   By kindness of the Public Record Office

4 Dealing with Crowd Disorders
   By kindness of the Public Record Office

5 Lists of Accused
   By kindness of the Public Record Office

6 Title Page, Zee-Roovers
   By kindness of the Trustees, British Museum

7 Pirate Raid on a Coastal Town (Zee-Roovers)
   By kindness of the Trustees, British Museum

8 The *Kingfisher* Action
   after Van der Velde the Younger
   By kindness of the Trustees, National Maritime Museum

End papers by Miss Jean Hooker

Photos 1*b*, 1*c*, 6 and 7 by Michael Ross-Wills of Millar and
Harris

Apart from illustrations 1*c* and 8, none of these illustrations
has appeared in a modern book

Acknowledgments

My deepest gratitude to:
The Lord Chancellor and the Lord Chief Justice for permission to photograph and reproduce the Admiralty Oar and modern Seal; to Kenneth Timings, Keeper (retired) of the Public Record Office, for having directed the writer to the little-known Admiralty Court Examinations and Acts of the sixteenth and seventeenth centuries; to Dr Cox of the Public Record Office for constant help and for his immense knowledge of PRO archives that made accessible the treasures mentioned in notes below the text.

I am deeply obligated to Mr Ricks, Admiralty Marshal, for his interest, patience and kind assistance.

Other acknowledgments will be found in the list of illustrations.

References

HCA = High Court of Admiralty
CSPD = Catalogue, State Papers Domestic

The writer has been informed by officials of the PRO that the Examinations and Acts quoted have not been examined previously.

PART I

I
Introduction

There exists an inferior painting (probably Italian) that has for a title: *And the sea gave up the dead which were in it.* The immensity of the theme belittles, especially, the painter's achievement—irresistibly touching off the question, What would Rembrandt or his equals have done with so majestic an idea? Still, bypassing such regrets in favour of the canvas that confronts us, we see, under a non-committal pale sky, a vast pale stretch of ocean, fading in the background to dimness. Out of this waste of water, forms animate and inanimate are rising. The foreground is dominated by a man in fifteenth-century dress, authoritative in his bearing, majestic in his sweeping scarlet cloak; most likely not a merchant, who would seldom take his wife along on a business trip, but a nobleman. His wife who rises beside him is beautifully dressed in pale cream. Both figures with hands crossed on their bosoms, with eyes serenely uplifted to heaven, are already clear of the water; the manner of both persons—a blend of pious humility combined with unmistakable confidence—suggests that they have no doubt of emerging well from the inquiries of the Heavenly Court.

The stretch of ocean behind them is variously broken by other emerging beings more and more shadowy as they retreat into the background, along with battered and dismasted ships likewise obeying the Last Trump. Among these wrecks appears an unmistakable trireme, irresistibly suggesting—for this gate-crasher of pre-Christian eras—some awkward moments in the court of the Christian Judge. But whether or no, the attention may now be taken by what is rising on the spectator's left, so shadowed and diminished by the foremost figures as to be scarcely visible, yet in it may lie the whole message and warning of the picture. This man, visible only so far as his waist, is barely covered by the few dirty rags which were evidently— from the example of the nobleman and lady—his apparel at the moment of death. His whole body, to judge by what can be seen, is already locked and twisted in agony, a spasm of apprehension and terror. His sins, whatever they were, have pounced the moment he got his head above water, nor will his convulsive and obvious desire to retreat again under the waves do him the least good against the power which is drawing him relentlessly to the surface. Yet if we ask what drowned man could emerge from the sea carrying with him so heavy a burden of crime, so black a consciousness of guilt, our choice might be of a pirate. Or rejecting this, we are constrained to wait till the Day of Judgment for the answer.

However, if the proceedings of the Heavenly Court are a little out of our reach, we are fortunate in possessing the records of a more earthly source: the Court of Admiralty. This body, founded in 1260, was of course running great guns at the period when English shipping was being most unceasingly and savagely attacked by pirates, a bar of judgment before which appeared, as mere daily routine, every blackest inhumanity, rapacity and violence, all powered by perhaps an even deeper guilt, the guilt of pre-intention: from the first moment of its existence completely knowing, and equally deliberate.

II

The Admiralty Court

The Court was already 295 years old (or nearly) by 1575, when our investigation begins. This particular interval, until 1675, is not a random choice, but is literally forced upon us by two elements: first, the decay of the Navy under the neglect and mishandling of James I, and second, by the corresponding, immediate and unprecedented growth of a piracy that not only harassed commerce on the seas around and far beyond England, but which overflowed into raids on coastal towns and villages, exclusively for the purpose of supplying an immense slave trade carried on mostly in Moroccan markets. This latter activity carries us into dimensions of misery, anguish, and ransom attempts both public and private beyond the scope of a single small book, perhaps beyond the scope of any book ever to be written. It would seem better, or at least within possibility of accomplishment, to attempt those Court proceedings that confined themselves to those crimes and felonies, alone, that made up the act of piracy as generally understood.

THE METHOD OF THE COURT

There appears to be in existence, according to expert opinion, no stenographer's record of Admiralty Court piracy proceedings: no word-for-word account of any trials or trials, from the preliminary Oyez, Oyez, to the final judgment. Yet, burrowing into the giant documentation that surrounds this curious emptiness, gradually the beginnings of suspicion take on the firmer outlines of conclusion: there are virtually no records of Court procedure because all the recording—essential and exclusive of the verdict—has been done *preliminary* to the Court sittings; and in such terrifying and voluminous detail that nothing is left for the Court but to observe the set formalities of swearing in the jury, reviewing for its benefit the nature of the accusation, and pronouncing sentence according to the jury's verdict. The number of cases one Justice could get through in a single day, as tabulated in the volumes called *Acts of Court*, indicate with what speed, and how efficiently, this method could be made to work. Nor in these whole proceedings of Admiralty, under its staggering case load, is there the slightest hint of carelessness, scanting or prejudice, and certainly not of vindictiveness. With dispatch yet with meticulous thoroughness the Court arrived at its judgments, confident in the weight of preliminary investigation of evidence; investigation massive, pitilessly detailed, and taken not before some minor judge or court official, but in the presence of an acting Justice of the High Court of Admiralty appointed to gather evidence.

The names of the preliminary documents on which the trial Justice based himself and the proceedings of his Court were as follows: Examinations; lists of jurors with addresses; Juratores; Presentments; warrants; columns of accused; after all this, a scattering of bits and scraps that sometimes convey information not given elsewhere. Of this whole collection, by far the most massive, detailed and important are the countless shabby volumes labelled Examinations.

EXAMINATIONS

Every page of these folio-sized books, thick and heavy, is crowded with the pale brown script of professional writers to the Court, taking down evidence as it came from the mouth of the examined. These entries include the witness's name, age, occupation and country of origin. If the witness has no English the fact is noted along with the name of an interpreter, plus the information that the interpreter has been sworn.

All the foregoing is in Latin; when the actual testimony begins, the language changes to English. And with this change there bursts from the written page a clamour of voices and presences alive and harsh, possessed by the injury they have suffered, by accusation, or by equal extremity of denying accusation; all these incandescent with hate or fogged with lies, evasions, contradictions, anything that gives the least hope of escape. It is this immediate living quality that overwhelms and impales one on the question: how have those people on the pages survived so long between the suffocating covers of a book?

How is it that the compressions of rage, desire of revenge, fear of revenge, have not ignited their receptacles and sent the volumes up in smoke? For—as may be gathered—the testimonies of pirates and of victims follow each other indiscriminately in the same book. Also, by the way, a great number of cases are years old, up to fifteen; it has taken an accident—the accident of capture—to land the pirates in the Admiralty dock, where their accusers can get at them at last. Any number of earlier cases involve piracies committed under Elizabeth I, yet never brought to trial until the early years of James I. The question of how the plundered merchants living at a distance— the Flemish, French, German, Dutch or Spanish— learned that the pirates were up for trial in London, comes up a little later.

The Examinations begin with a first statement from the witness, whether a robbed merchant, his crew members or passengers, or from the company of the pirate ship. As far as can be told from the nature of these testimonies, the narrator was uninterrupted—at this point—by questioning, challenging, or severities of any kind. However long this initial statement— and some of them run to six or eight closely written folio pages —the witness is free, in every respect, to go his own gait.

The first statement is now over; especially after a long one or even a fairly long one, the testifier may be looked upon as pretty well exhausted. It is precisely at this point that the examining Judge drops on him with the second part of the ordeal. This is called the Interrogatory, and consists of a merciless review of every statement the witness has made, with the most grinding and detailed inquisition concerning it. It may be conjectured that most witnesses were unprepared for this excruciating corollary; quite unaware, all the time, that the sting was in the tail. As to how many errors were exposed in this manner, how many inaccuracies deliberate or accidental, how many lying witnesses trapped in their lies, conjecture itself staggers. It seems that the English mind has a peculiar genius which turns into a trap; one remembers the report of Henry VIII's inquisitors: 'We have so entangled her that she will never get free of it.' In this business of Interrogatories many witnesses judged too unimportant to bother with escaped the process altogether, but not the principals; never the principals.

A word might be said, at this point, of the person who

conducted the Examinations early in the 1600s, the famous
Justice, Sir Julius Caesar of the Admiralty Court. One perceives
(or fancies) an additional quality of deadliness and pointedness
in his Interrogatories; and here we must remember that the
Justice apparently had no set form of questioning to use, but had
to derive his inquiries, individually, from the witness's first
statement. Of what power of concentration this implies, of what
lethal patience and grim attention, it is impossible now to
estimate; yet if the Interrogatory did not take from the Judge
its peculiar and overwhelming quality of relentlessness, it is
difficult to imagine where the credit should go.

LISTS OF JURORS

These endless columns of names plus addresses will be found not
only with other material in the volumes of Court procedure
called *Acts*, but also in various compilations of documents that
have only a class mark to distinguish them. The property or
means of these candidates for jury duty, which alone qualifies
them as eligible, are never mentioned in these lists, but of
course have been ascertained in advance and registered elsewhere. Some lists are short, a dozen to twenty names; others,
much longer, seem to indicate both a busy time coming up in the
Admiralty Court, and trials of greater importance.

JURATORES

The single word in black imperious lettering at once directs the
attention to those who will try the case. Declining at once to
the ordinary writing of court scribes, in brief professional terms
and without waste of words the document lays open the wound
of accusation before those who, in the end, will bear the heavy
responsibility of the verdict. This item of the legal machinery,
which defines and explains the case that the jury will have to
consider, is always written entirely in Latin and on parchment
(lists of jurors, for example, are always on poor quality paper).
Most Juratores are limited to one long paragraph on a folio
page thriftily cut in half, but there exist examples occupying
a full folio sheet of parchment in the case of multiple accusations
with their varying details.

The existence of these Juratores arouses curiosity as to Court procedure. Every juryman could read and write, assuredly, and every school of standing started its pupils with Latin, but what degree of skill in it did these solid tradesmen retain? Did the trial therefore open with a reading of the Juratores first in the original, then in English? This would seem absolutely essential. Did the Judge then invite questions from those jurymen who were still not quite certain of what they had heard? Again this would seem a step of procedure impossible to omit.

Again, the material of accusation contained in the Juratores could only have been drawn up by skilled lawyers attached to the Court; material out of the Examinations, distilled and compressed, from which every irrelevance has been purged so that the juror's attention could rest, entirely, on those aspects of the charge from which their decision would be drawn. And from the final development of every trial that has ever been held—the verdict—it will be surprisingly evident that Admiralty juries were not to be swayed or overpowered by any presiding judge; of those juries, docility or cowardice were not conspicuous qualities.

PRESENTMENTS, PRECEPTS AND WARRANTS

The modest-sized documents called Presentments simply listed the names of persons coming up for trial, with a description of their (alleged) misdemeanours. Here they are, they say silently, now get to work on them, and having done this much are silent.

Any comment on seventeenth-century Warrants must be preceded by mention of what was apparently an earlier form of Warrant: the Precept. This is still defined in law as an Order: the hairline between it and a Warrant, which is an authorisation, is too subtle for the untrained mind to define. If Precepts were an accepted form of Warrant early in the sixteenth century, by the end of it they were beginning to be scarce, at least in the HCA volumes consulted. Of the only three examples found in the last quarter of the 1500s, one is a Precept (1577) for the execution of 'Roland Blevyn et alteri' for piracy, followed by an Indenture (5 July 1577) for transfer of the same persons from one prison to another. A second Precept (1578) is for execution of 'Robert Hicks et alteri, for piracy against a hoy of Yarmth'; the hoy is a comedown for Hicks, who earlier has been up for piracy on three ships.* A third Precept (date illegible) is for execution of 'Vincent Cavard et al'. The hasty assumption that the term so used has become obsolete in the seventeenth century is considerably shaken by discovery of a Precept dated 28 March 1605, but this one is not for ordinary execution, but for the terrible sentence called *peine forte et dure*. In fact the Precept is a form still used in law, perhaps not very often.

The Warrant itself, on the other hand, had unlimited uses; it could be framed to meet any occasion or any contingency, from the gravest down to the most petty. Being in any context an attestation or affirmation of fact, one class of Warrant gives the person who holds it—by the mere fact of his being named to hold it—certain definite powers to carry out its instructions, at the same time imposing limitations on the powers so conferred.

The Warrants applicable to the crime of piracy, however, begin by referring to the arrest of persons so accused, progress to the matter of bail if granted or detention in gaol if not granted, and from there proceed to the trial and the verdict. The most interesting Warrants of the historic area under scrutiny of course pertain to characters whose acquaintance we have made in the Examinations, and whose infamy, cruelty or inhumanity we have been able to accept or not accept, according to the evidence. As to the results of the trial, we have hundreds of trial warrants on the backs of which someone has written the jury's verdict *Ignoramus* (we don't know); this would certainly mean acquittal. Also in hundreds of cases (written at the back or at the foot of Warrants) there are solid indications that the accused will be executed, but again there exist countless numbers in which is given no indication of the final outcome; none at all. We must reckon ourselves likewise with the destructive gaps in the narrative; if the Examinations are so fascinating that one can hardly wait for the trial, the trial turns up missing; if the trial itself is especially evocative, the Examination cannot be traced. The present research has not succeeded in finding an unbroken account of the preliminary Examination, trial and execution of a single pirate, only some incomplete steps which break off just as they excite the greatest curiosity.

* HCA 1-2/76-8

We may take it for granted, however—from the mere volume of work churned out by the Admiralty Court—that the gallows of Wapping and Southwark were kept busy. We may also assume, from the evidence of the Examinations, that the men who decorated these contrivances were ferocious brutes indifferent to what savagery of maltreatment they inflicted, so long as they could get their claws on a ship's cargo.

It is necessary to mention the rigorous yet humane practice of the Admiralty Court in granting bail to so many men who were to stand trial—and who, once they were on trial, ended on the gallows not only for piracy, but for murder committed in the course of piracy. Yet such stories, as they begin in the Examinations, may be so clouded with ignorance real or pretended, that they give no indication of the waiting horror till some weak link in the chain—some witness terrified, exhausted or otherwise vulnerable—lets it slip out.

All this time a single query, unforeseen, is giving rise to more and more dissatisfaction. Where are the Warrants for execution? How explain their scarcity? After months of dogged search for such documents, there appear only two instances of what one might call a substitute warrant, in that the conclusion—or the allusion rather—is unmistakable.

The first instance,* undated and without signature or seals, is plainly a memorandum: 'Johannes Gryffyn piratt, Robertus piratt [sic] and William Clerke piratt [are condemned] to a public death, and to your custody the said piratts are comitted.' At the bottom of the page, a brief postscript: 'As regards the said Robert piratt: hee on his said arrival to suffer the said punishment.' The writer, disturbed perhaps by the absence of Robert's family name, appears to be making sure of him by a process of double nailing.

The second example, even further from a writ of execution, is nevertheless informative on the atmosphere created by public hangings. Perfectly divorced from the stately and ceremonious dispatch of nobles male or female, these turnings-off of low grade thieves, pirates and murderers must have convened crowds similarly low grade, and—it goes without saying— enormous. Of such scum with their gleeful ferocity of appetite for the spectacle, their deafening cheers, shrieks and catcalls as

* HCA 3, 3, p. 20

the cart with the condemned was fighting its way towards the gallows, the senseless violence ready to explode into attempts to rescue the prisoners—of these and worse the authorities must have had a bellyful, to judge by the tone of the following (1610):* 'Whereas certain piratts condemped for piracy are to be executed at morninge on Saturday the XIIJ of this instant moneth of October: These are to require and chardge you on his Ma^ts behaulfe, to take care that a sufficant garde of honest inhabitants nere Wappinge be provided and be ready at the place of execution in fare tyme as the said piratts are to suffer death, to see the paire dropte; and that no disorder hinder. And that his Ma^ts service be done, faile ye not; as you tender [respect?] his Ma^ts service and will answere the contrary, at your uttermost perile. From the Doctors Comons.' No signature to this, and no seal.

The two above examples, however, remain not genuine warrants, but mere testimony of execution. For the entire absence of proper warrants, however, the explanation may be simple. The person of the pirate to be hanged would be accompanied by a proper warrant from the Admiralty Court to the local sheriff charged with the hanging, in the fullest correctitude of English law. After the execution this warrant would be returned via the sheriff to the Court, with a note signifying the carrying out of the sentence. But the Admiralty Court archives were by no means for the preservation of testimony relating to the lowest of the low; they had more important evidences to worry about. Perhaps the document was destroyed directly, upon receipt. What tracks these hanged men have left are vocal: their own testimony and the testimony of witnesses, in volumes of Examinations. They are also fleetingly alive in Presentments, Precepts or Warrants. Apparently we are bound to be grateful for what we have, while cherishing the sneaking hope: that the annals of survival are perfect caverns of secrecy, which sometimes disgorge—without rhyme or reason—the most shattering proofs and testimonies of past events. It may be that some fortunate seeker will at some time turn up a pirate's warrant of execution, for the tale of survival, among all strange tales, is one of the strangest.

It might be mentioned here that the Admiralty Court,

* HCA 1–6

staggering under its terrific schedule of maritime cases criminal and non-criminal, is trying to lighten its load. From about 1606 to 1608 arrangements are made to have pirates tried at any court of Assize nearest the scene of their capture, thus avoiding the trouble and expense of getting them to London under guard, the issuing of warrants, and what not. The earliest ruling of these provisions is, that any pirate case can be tried by such courts excepting those involving deaths, whether by accident or murder. In a very short time, however, this condition was rescinded, and we have inferior courts imposing the death sentence and indeed—in at least one case—the horrific sentence of *peine forte et dure.*

Public Advertisement of Trial

At a time when there were few newspapers to carry public announcements of any sort, and when the desperate slowness both of national and overseas transport might impede such intelligence until too late to act on, one may wonder at the immense number of Hollandish, French, German, Spanish and other merchants who thronged the Admiralty Court. Moreover, such plaintiffs usually brought with them a number of witnesses whose expenses they bore, naturally; and since most of such witnesses did not speak English, it is conceivable that the plaintiff not only had the responsibility of finding an interpreter acceptable to the Court, but of paying his fees likewise.

Yet, in spite of the enormous difficulties they faced on every hand, such plaintiffs and their accompaniments did turn up and, moreover, turned up in time for trial. How did they manage it? How did they get word of the date of sittings, at a period when the imagination faints at thought of the difficulties involved?

If conjecture enters here, again, again it must be forgiven. As for notifying Dutch merchants in piracy or other cases, it is difficult to avoid giving some credit—at least—to the Steelyard. This tremendous Hollandish organization, London-based, probably had facilities for getting news as promptly as possible to its members living abroad, or perhaps it maintained a list of its non-member countrymen who had suffered piracy. If the Fuggers could maintain a news agency plus a messenger service second to none, why not a wealthy company like the Steelyard?

For the non-members a fee would probably be charged for such notification, but for those who paid the regular membership subscription, probably nothing. This is at least a reasonable guess for the presence of foreign-based merchants in such crowds at the Admiralty Court, and would seem to be confirmed merely by glancing at the Steelyard officials. Self-possessed, hard as nails yet well-bred, immensely intelligent, they look at you from the canvases that do full justice to their clothes, severe and sober and obviously expensive.

As for French, German and Spanish merchants, we can only assume that their friends in London would notify them, as quickly as possible, of the dates of Court sittings. But with the English plaintiffs, at once we are on firm ground. Sittings of various Courts were advertised by bills publicly posted; of these, few traces survive. One example* is a writ or mandate, appointing 'tryalls to be held at Southwarke on Tuesday 10 June 1634, for all occasions of piratical robbery or spoyling', and for all 'who have occasion of complaints to make their appearance, and bring such evidences as they shall think fitt.' The writ also specifies, 'We will and require you to affixx this mandate uppon some eminent place of our Royall Exchange, London, at the usuall tyme of resort of merchants thither'.

The second such advertisement was written on the back of a warrant announcing a trial of pirates on 24 November 1634, 'at his Ma^tys Court of Admiraltie:† A Summons for all such as have been robbed, spoyled or wronged by any of the pirats nowe in prison.' Below it is the directive 'to putt this notice upp at the Royall Exchange', and beneath this again, 'This warrant was fixxed in the Royall Exchange the 25th, 27th and 29th of Novemb^r by me, William Pope.'

Both these examples seem of a rather late period; if earlier ones exist, the present research has missed them.

* HCA 1–7—75/107
† HCA 1–7—64/114

III
Straight Piracies

For the sudden and enormous increase of pirate cases in the Admiralty Court from 1602, there is one good and famous reason: the early action of King James I, characteristically half-witted, in cancelling all further protective action by naval patrols, and in recalling all such ships into port. The grapevine grew powerfully; in no time at all after this edict the ocean was alive with pirate craft, seeking whom they might devour. Of an equally terrible consequence, the coastal pirate raids that kidnapped men, women and children for the Moroccan slave markets, there is no room except for mere mention; our present concern is the pirates' effect on commerce.

By 'straight piracy' is meant the common or garden variety of sea-pillage—violence solely to cargoes, which took place without attendant circumstances of serious bodily injury or death. The numbers of such robberies (mostly by English pirates) upon French, Venetian, Spanish, Breton, Flemish and Hollandish merchant ships must mount, between the seventeenth and early eighteenth centuries, into thousands and perhaps tens of thousands. And though the bloodless piracy did not inflict physical cruelties, yet the viva voce testimony of those who suffered in a day when there existed no system of insurances, no compensation of any kind, is sparked with that bitterness of loss, that durable rancour of serious money injury along with the memory of helplessness under such injury—which in any age or language must strike a note familiar to any ear, and no less recognisable than familiar.

However, before proceeding to these varied and justified discords of resentment, we must consider some aspects of the stage on which they were set. All the plundered ships cited here were in size between 100 and 180 tons; merchant ships seem to have been no bigger. This matter of size was always scrupulously noted in the Inquiratur, along with her name, her home port, the name of her owner or owners, the names of her captain

and crew, from what port to what port she was bound, and to
what extent she was armed. Then with painstaking detail her
cargo was described, and only after all this was disposed of were
the witnesses called up one by one, sworn, and examined. The
examiner (as has been mentioned) was always a Justice of the
Admiralty Court, and his examination was mercilessly thorough
and unhurried. If dissatisfied with any part of it (as has been
mentioned) he might grind what was left of the wretched
witness into dust, by means of the Interrogatory. The volumes
of Examinations preserve not only the voices of the injured;
they stand as a memorial to the quality and the hard work of the
examining Admiralty Judges. In volume HCA–34 one such
character so presents himself in his formidable panoply of
persistence and skill in taking a witness to pieces as to outrank—
or apparently—other examining Justices. If the thousands of
grillings have exaggerated to one person this quality of cold
yet ferocious patience, apologies are unreservedly offered. Yet
every re-examination of the testimony so overawes with its icy
power of intent, its pitiless legalistic hunt for truth, as to compel
a few lines for the bygone creator of this atmosphere.

Justice Sir Julius Caesar (1557–1636)

The classical spelling of his name, which he obviously preferred,
is sometimes found in the Examinations as Sezar. His father
was physician to queens Mary and Elizabeth. He took his BA
and MA at Oxford, and at twenty-five was admitted member of
the Inner Temple. Next he went abroad, and in 1581 took his
doctorate of law in Paris. He returned to England, by 1584 was
made a Judge of the Admiralty Court, and was knighted by
James in 1603. This was by no means his only dignity—he was
appointed Chancellor and Under-Treasurer of the Exchequer in
1606—but the volumes of Admiralty Examinations, unmentioned in any account of his life that the present writer has
ever seen, perhaps remain as his unequalled memorial. It seems
that he was strikingly generous to the poor, even beyond the
call of religion or duty, and had attractive qualities of friendship;
that unpleasant great man, Francis Bacon, was an admirer of his.
He made his eighty, dying in 1636. Not only was his climb

steady and unclouded, but he left a considerable fortune to his son, Charles.

THE CASES

The following major robbery,* by thoroughpaced professional pirates, has some unusual features. (23 April 1600): 'Examination of John Seline of Brest, mariner, in the ship the *Trinity* of Brest, through an interpreter sayeth: that on the last day of December last he, being bound for Marcelles [Marseilles] in the *Trinity*, of which he was owner, was chased when on the quost [coast] of Spaine by two shippes, from about midday to midnighte. Whereof one of them came upp with this ex^{ate} [examinate] about midnighte, and tooke him. And they comanded him to speke, both in ffrench and spanishe. [But] shortly after, this ex^{ate} herde them speke Englishe, and tooke them for Englishe.'

Poor John, he concluded too soon that his troubles were over.

'And said, he hoped they would trete him well, for that he had pasport from the Lord High Admiral of Englande, for that viadge [voyage].'

Much good this did him.

'Then a greate number of men aborded him, and putt this ex^{ate} and all his company under hatches, and there kepte them fowre and twenty houres as prisoners.'

Apparently this imprisoning of the crew, while they ransacked the ship at their leisure, was a standard technique of less sanguinary pirates; at least it was assurance of a sort that the intention was not to capture and sell them into slavery. In this instance, with all possible interference cooped up below, the captors were having a wonderful time—how wonderful John knew, to an unendurable degree. Here the writer begs forgiveness if the descriptions of victualling and cargo seem too many or too detailed; yet to one person at least they speak in their way of the marvellous textures of life, of manifold skill in manufactures, from those of plainest utility to the most luxurious and extravagant. In the case of the *Trinity*, she comes about half way between the highest and lowest degree, laden as

* HCA 1–2—194B

she is with articles of practical necessity—their variety and their fate, both, in John's own words.

'They rifled the shipp and caried away into their shipp fyve balles [bales] of dowlas [coarse linen imported from Brittany], every balle conteyning VIII peeces and a haulfe; two other packes of dowlas; Six smale balles of dowlas peeces. fourteene thousand dry fyshe, 2 kintalles [quintals: can also mean 100 pounds]. ordinance of Iron with their cariges, wheyinge XXXCL [300 lb.]. Two cables wheyinge CC lb, one haulser of XXC lb wayght, a boat with mast, sailes and oars. Four pipes and a haulfe of bread and other loose bread to the quantity of twenty kintalles, thre hogsheads of beefe, thre hogheds of meale, two hundred and a haulfe of powder, two dozen of pikes, ten musketts and thre Calvers and their furniture [French blunderbusses and their ammunition]. a kintall of candelles, one kintall of wax, twenty potts of butter, four hundred wayght of cordage with pullies, plus the mariners apparell, it being wintere; two compasses and two hourglasses, XIII swordes. And so,' he winds up, 'they departed.'

Now, shut up below, they waited a cautious period of time 'till they heard no noise above,' John continues, 'and then lifted upp the hatches and came upp. And founde all the Englishmen gone and all the goodes taken away and nothinge left, but some residew of the ladinge, being fyshe. And so he was enforced,' he concludes bitterly, 'to putt into Spaine, being spoyled of his victualls, also of his shipps furniture.'

At this point we have something as remarkable as rare— nothing less than a confrontation. The piracy had taken place only four months ago, yet already the pirates had been captured; two of them (Rombles and Sackeld) were now produced before John, who identified them at once. 'He sayeth he *certainly* knoweth the two persons, and that they came on borde the *Trinity* with the rest that spoyled him, as aforesaid.'

Moreover he can testify to an especially flagrant act, before he and his crew were driven under hatches. 'He sayeth the lesser of them brake open his cheste and tooke out the pasport of the Lord High Admirale in this ex^ates presence,' and adds that 'more over, before he was shutt upp, he took such weare [awareness, notice] of them that he knoweth them very well.'

The next person heard—Eyvan Hugan of Brest—is pilot of

the plundered ship, and turns out to be as formidable a witness as his employer. He adds some details: that the pirates 'shott two peeces of ordinance and musketts' before boarding the *Trinity*, and that first they tried to pass themselves off as Spanish, then as French. Eyvan is also responsible for a pleasant story; when one of the looters shouted down and threatened them 'if they wld not confesse where the rest of the goodes were, answere came upp to them: that yf they had not all the goodes, they might seeke for them.' After citing this spirited retort, Eyvan confirms John's sinister recognition of the two prisoners: 'he tooke such notice of them when they came on borde, that he verie well knoweth them', and adds a detail: 'he sawe the lesser of the two persons layinge against the mast, and comanded others to rast [roust out] fowre of the fyshe.' The memory rankled, evidently—the sight of this bandit taking it easy and having a little picnic on his own. Moreover he confirms the theft of the passport by 'the lesser p'son', adds his opinion that this lesser person was captain of the pirates, and concluded desolately: 'They left behind them nothinge, not soe much as a kniffe to call their owne or a cann to drinke with; and besides did beate and insult them verie badly, and he him selfe is not yett whole.'*

Testimony from other *Trinity* seamen goes to show that their ages run from thirty to fifty; a sober professional outfit, most of them in the employ of John Seline for a number of years.

This next piracy is big-time, involving seventy attackers, and is likewise remarkable on three other counts. First there was involved a really great sum of money aboard, something not so usual; second, there will appear a lamentation for something not tangible, yet of boundless price and estimate to one possessor; third, the frantically awkward revelation that lies beneath it all. The date of the hearing is 23 April 1600, the ship was the *Mary* (French); the examinate was John Cromer, merchant and co-owner of the *Mary*, which evidently specialized—in a big way—in cargoes of spices, foodstuffs, and other domestic consignments.

John, carefully retracing 'the spoyle don upon the *Mary*'

---

* Threatening and beating is so frequently charged against pirates that the offence congealed into a set form in the indictment: 'Insultam et affraiam fecerint, verbarint et maletractarint, ita quod de vitis eorum desperabantur.'

first describes how in December 1599 at 'Allicaunte [Alicante] she laded fifty six butts of sweete oyle, thre little barrelles of sweete oyle and one tonne and a haulfe of rape' plus 'capers and wheate. And sayled from thence, 'he continues, 'to a roade called Shabye, and there this ex^{ate} bought and laded fifteene tonnes of rise [rice], two tonnes and a haulfe of soape [Queen Elizabeth had made cleanliness fashionable], a bagge or aniseede, VIII tonnes of salte and a tonne of wine. All for the accompte', he reminds us, 'of the ex^{ate} and his partners.'

After all this buying and selling John was left with what must always have been a gnawing worry—the safe disposition of his cash.

'Having nineteene bagges of Rialles of plate (reales of silver), every bagge conteyninge one hundred crownes,' he explains, 'and fowr hundred and threscore crownes in goulde left from the sale of the goodes outward caried, this ex^{ate} hid the same bagges in a secrete place of the shippe.'

This was only the beginning.

'And thre hundred crownes in goulde he hid in another place, and kepte aboute him one hundred and ten crownes in gould. And then,' he explains, as if in afterthought, 'fifteen eand fifty crownes of gould he hid in another place of the said shipp. And beinge come aboute fifty leages of the Roche [Rock]—' one feels the cruel thrust and lightning-stroke of misfortune '— they sawe an englishe shipp pursuing them, which she did for aboute two houres space.'

The *Mary*, which had a total crew of fourteen men and two boys and also carried some small armament of cannon and weapons, was not going to give up at once.

'Shee shott at the *Mary*, greate shott,' John deposes, 'and the *Mary* shott agains, and the two shippes foughte together aboute an hower.' But the outcome was never in doubt. 'The *Mary* having yelded, then,' he continues, 'LXX men entered into her oute of the englishe shipp, which was called the *Swann*.'

The plundering of cargo began at once—naturally—yet in all the uproar a small element of misgiving and uncertainty was beginning to insinuate itself. John had managed, then or later, to pick up a few names of the unwelcome visitors. 'John Martyn was captaine of the *Swann*,' he notes, 'one Spicer was m^r, and one Midleton was a gent.'

Of this 'gent' species of seaman, more later; the tale approaches its crux with, 'One John Newport was leftenant.'

It is this Newport who begins giving the game away; loot or no loot, he cannot but be aware of something unpleasant developing in the situation. He asked John if they were not Frenchmen; when the answer was yes, he must have blenched. France and England were at peace, and under Elizabeth—of all sovereigns—this status quo was disturbed only at the disturber's risk. Evidently, confronting this unpleasant truth, Newport lost his nerve all at once.

'He instantly disalowed the facte (repudiated the capture)' John recounts, and blamed the captaine for medling with us,' then followed this up by going to the captain and demanding that he let the prize go free. The suggestion, however, did not come at the best moment; both captain and crew were in the full bliss of gutting the *Mary*. From that moment however, and to his credit, Newport never ceased to protest their depredations, nor to obstruct other lethal proposals at every turn, as much as he could. And even if his zeal were only fired by the customary devotion to one's own neck, it seems not discreditable in the circumstances.

Meanwhile the pirates had begun transferring cargo from the *Mary* to the *Swan*, and not only cargo. 'They pillaged the most parte of the almondes and soape,' testifies John, 'together with two smale cases of silke and a cheste of Looking glasses. And stripped the marriners of all their apparell to their shirts [in December] and caried them into the *Swann*. And—'

At this point, with apologies, we interrupt his rising voice for the briefest possible comment. A good deal is known about successful merchants of that time; how they dressed and what impression they made. We have seen the Steelyard merchants in indoor dress; in winter such men would wear a heavy greatcoat lined with rabbit or squirrel reaching to the ankles, and with lynx, wolf or fox fur at the neck and wrists, and our John—having to meet his peers at every port, also making an ocean voyage in December—would not be less impressively got up. Therefore we understand his note of outrage as he describes how, as well as his men, he too was 'sente abord the *Swann* in his shirte, clapped and spoyled of all his apparell in most turkish and barbarous maner. Which grieved him,' he adds, on a top note of sincerity, 'more than the losse of his goodes.'

After this the whole affair sails rapidly toward revelation and disaster. By now the *Swan* is bound for England, with part of its crew bringing the *Mary* along in its wake. Meanwhile John, still imprisoned aboard the *Swan*, can easily hear vociferations going on—arguments increasing in turbulence and anger, as more and more of the crew begin to share Newport's uneasiness. Has the capture of the *Mary* been in fact illegal, to say nothing of the thieving and other damage done by the *Swan*? Are all of them sailing toward calamity, in plain language the gallows? Two new ideas are proposed: make at once for Barbary and sell the *Mary*'s goods, the *Mary*'s crew and the *Mary* herself; or, alternatively, transfer *Mary*'s whole cargo into the *Swan* and sink the *Mary*. 'Which in this ex^ates opinion they had don,' John testifies—except that the usual obstacle interposed itself. 'Newport would not suffer them therein.' By this time Newport must have had a good part of the crew backing him up. In this highly disturbing muddle they put in at St Ives in Cornwall— from sheer fright presumably, also for time to settle their differences—and hustled John 'a shere [shore] and kepte him in a house there, for fyve days.'

By this time, apparently, they had agreed on a course of action. First they released John who did not seem, then or later, properly grateful; later on he picked up a rumour that the *Mary* had been 'brought to the key [quay] and all her goodes landed.' This of course meant that the captors had braced themselves to put a legal face on the affair, and were landing the captured cargo for the first necessary step—the Queen's valuation. Here John's testimony ends. Curiously, he has said nothing about the great sums of money secreted in the *Mary*—which does not mean that we shall be deprived, altogether, of the clink and gleam of gold.

The next witness, on the same date, was Martyn Dales, pilot of the *Mary*. His comment on the capture of the *Mary* is repetitious, but couched in beautiful (also heroic) seaman's language: 'Uppon first sighte of the *Swann* she was fule in the wind, and we wente before the winde. And perceyving the *Swann* to be a man of Warre, the witness and company p'vided themselves to fight [bravo]. And the *Swann* came upp in short space with the *Mary*.'

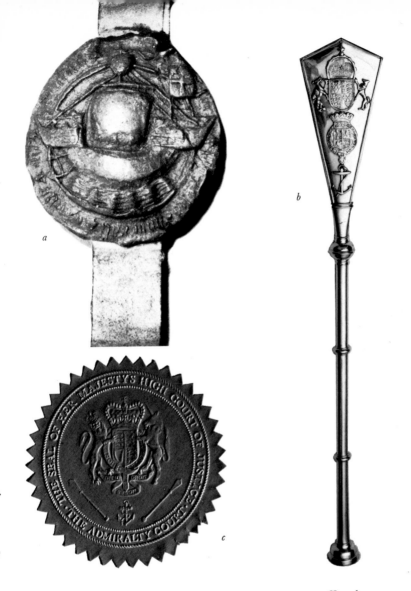

1 *a* Seal, possibly from the fourteenth century, affixed to a warrant of appointment. *b* The Oar, formerly placed before the President during sittings of Court. The silver blade dates from James II; the loom, of iron sheathed in silver, is hall-marked 1798–99. *c* Admiralty Seal with Fouled Anchor, from accession of Elizabeth II.

2 Indictment (partial) *Peine forte et dure*: '. . . stones and iron shalbe placed over him, and when he drinks he shall not eat, and when he eats he shall not drink'

3 *Warrant for peine forte et dure*, in the name of Charles Earl of
Nottingham, with his seal

4 Dealing with crowd disorders: 'Whereas certain piratts are to be executed . . . these are to require of you a sufficient garde.' (from Doctors Commons)

DE
AMERICAENSCHE
ZEE-ROOVERS
Behelsende een Partinent
Verhael van alle de Roverye
En Onmenselÿcke Vreet-
heeden die de Engelsche
en Franse Roovers
Tegens de Spanjaerden
in America
Gepleeght
Hebben.

6   *The Fascinating Subject*: written *ca.* 1675, published 1678

7 Pirates' Raid on a Coastal Town, *ca.* 1670 (Zee-Roovers)

8 *HMS Kingfisher* attacking seven pirate ships. Engraving after Van der Velde the Younger (seventeenth century)

Now something interesting.

'Wee herde the trumpette sound [from the *Swann*: the signal to attack] and a peece of ordinance came over us, but without doinge any harme to the *Mary*.'

Any good sized ship armed for attack or defence gave her orders by trumpet-blast; the trumpeter is always present on such craft.

'This witness comaunded his company not to shoote,' Martyn continues, 'but to see further what they would doe.'

'What they would doe' was to send over a second shot, which hit; again the trumpet was heard, and a third and fourth shot came over the *Mary*. Besides an account of this instrumental prelude, Martyn includes a bitter listing of his own pilfered wardrobe: 'two old doublettes, a mandilion [a long jacket: obs.] and a cloke.' He strenuously denies [and we believe him] that he had ever betrayed the fact of money hidden in the ship: 'for that uppon notice of yt,' he says reasonably, 'he feared yt would all be lost.'

The next witness is a surprise: none other than the captain of the *Swan*, John Martyn. Still, as this case is not straightforward piracy but is also entangled with a breach of the international code—and also with another embarrassment still to be revealed —it is perhaps inevitable that he should be examined, and with such ferocious thoroughness that he appears, at times, more or less inside-out. It is no injustice to say that, in the chief part of his statement, he is lying from start to finish.

'He sayeth he first escried the *Mary* betwixt the Rock and cape pitcher. The *Mary* had XX men and boyes in her when he took the same, and the *Swann* had betwixt threscore and forescore men in her.' He follows this with an admission, dangerous: 'It is true that John Cromer owner of the *Mary*, tould him they were ffrench, and the goodes belonged to ffrench men.' Now commanded to name his master, pilot and other officers he does so, but begins to hesitate when he comes to a certain group of six. Urged along harshly by Justice Caesar he admits, awkwardly enough, that 'they were in the nature of gentlemen therein'. This returns us to that earlier mention of 'one Midleton, gent.'

It was a quite common thing for non-pirates to buy into a professional pirate cruise in hopes of extravagant profits ahead.

That they were also buying into prospects of being hanged was undeniable, but perhaps less regarded. Quite possibly these adventurous sprigs were, in actuality, gentlemen; Martyn, under pressure, admits that Robert Biddale, Rowland Powell, John Brook and others had invested money in the *Swan's* voyage, 'but he remembereth not, what every one of them adventured', though he does recollect that the *Swan's* master was in it for the sum of ten pounds.

Now, having made Judge Caesar's life difficult with his uncertainties, he abandons semi-falsehood for an article slightly less spurious. 'He haled the ffrench shipp 3 times and shott *one* peece over her to cause her to yelde, then the *Mary* shott our foremast clene through.' [Cheers for the *Mary*.] 'And the ffrench shipp begunn to fight [iniquitous of him certainly] for *he* shott only one shott', and having established his reasonable nature, he descends again to barefaced lying. 'He sayeth he shipped not any of the ffrench men; whether some of his company shipped any of them, he knoweth not.' A likely statement. Next he alibis himself for the stealing of clothes: if the French appeared half-naked, it was because 'he understood that most of them shapped [stripped] themselves into their shirtes, ready to fyghte.' In December? Moreover, his restraint was such that he never boarded the *Mary* till much later. '*He* wente not aborde her till 3 howers after the fyghte. And so,' he peeps, 'he knoweth not what chistes they broke open or what pilladge they had, but he had 2 looking glasses from 2 of the company.'

Here it is a pity that we cannot supply the Judge's harsh questioning, which must have battered against him all this while; all we know is that—at this point—he was suddenly hounded into a first, highly qualified reference to the money hidden aboard.

'In foule weather,' he admits, '2 little bagges of canvas fell oute of a hole in the cabon, which the [*Swan's*] m^r tooke upp. And this ex^ate tooke yt from him and opened yt, and therein were forty fyve Crownes in pistoletts and fyve or six peeces of sylver. Which,' he asserts, with reviving virtue, '*he* had not, for his parte,' and goes on to assert that the *Mary's* owner (Cromer) 'was not kepte as a prisoner at St Ives, but rather as. a gent. And confesseth he sente the sd Cromer to London.'

Obviously paying his expenses as amends, also in hopes of softening his evidence at the trial.

All this time, again, Judge Caesar must have bored unceasingly at the question of the *Swan*'s ownership, and again Martyn must have held him off as long as possible. Now, all at once, his resistance collapses.

'The Earle of Cumberland is owner of the *Swann*, to his knowledge.'

Here we may imagine a slight silence of consternation; Martyn follows it up with an admission even worse.

'He had not any Letters of Reprisall under the Seale of the Admiralty.'

Hastily he tries to patch this with another statement: 'He referreth to the Comission taken oute by the Earle of Cumberland', but is evidently aware that this will not help much. By now the fifteenth question of the Interrogatory is put to him, but he is too unmistakably weary to remember much. 'He sayeth there is Rice, sope, wine and other goodes in the *Mary*, but what the quantity is, he knoweth not.'

His signature to this, for all his fatigue, is a clear educated one.

No more is heard of this case; understandably it came up in Council, with Elizabeth's piercing voice heading the general condemnation. It could not have gone very well for Cumberland —owner of a ship that attacked the vessels of friendly powers, and had not even the legality of Letters of Reprisal to justify the action. The affair must have got into the records of Privy Council.

Will someone look?

No worse could happen to a merchant ship being chased by pirates, unless she were chased at the same moment by two pirates. The examination of Antonio de Morera, master (by interpreter) tells us of the fate of the '*St Anthony* of Luxborne, Portugall, 80 tonnes, laden at ffarnambuck [Farnambuco] with suger, brasill wood and sucketts [dried plums]'. As it happened the cargo on this particular leg of the voyage was not of great value; yet the ship carried for one of her size, and as part of her permanent fittings, a considerable armament. This Antonio describes: 'he had on borde XX fightinge men, ten musketts, a

faulconet [small cannon], XXX pounds of powder and seven
bales of wild fier, and fyve or six rapiers.'

'The sixte of May last,' he continues, 'aboute fyve of the clocke
in the morninge, he escried a great shipp giving him chase,
which pursued him an hower more or less. Noe other shipp was
then in sight,' he adds, giving a sudden vision of sea-emptiness
and men thrown unsparingly back on their own resources. Yet
suddenly a smaller ship, a caravel 'bearing to southwarde'
appeared out of nowhere. A possible ally, the reader hopes?
Anything but.

'The Caravel cast aboute and came bearinge round uppon this
ex^{ate}, and,' Antonio continues, 'the greater shipp did still the
like.' This double pursuit went on 'fower houres more or less,
and the great shipp made a shott at this ex^{ate}, which grased
[grazed] him. But the Carvel being the nerer to this ex^{ate}, put
out her oares and rowed towardes him.'

As nasty a situation as possible, then a sudden turn of affairs.

'This ex^{ate}, seeinge he should be taken, determined to yelde
rather to the greater shipp than to the lesser. And so caused the
pilot to beare towardes the greater shipp with his sailes full
spred, seeing the Carvel rowing full uppon him.'

Alas, too soon it was evident that his plan was not going to
work; the caravel was much closer to him than the bigger ship.
At his word of command the pilot left the wheel, 'and he and all
his company putt them selves under hatches. But,' he hangs on to
his pride, 'we *still* stroke not our sailes, at all.'

Almost at once, from below, they could hear the racket of the
caravel's men boarding the ship and starting the usual ruinous
hunt and havoc among the cargo. In no time at all, likewise,
they heard the advent of new arrivals—the company of the
bigger ship arriving and demanding their share, in no uncertain
terms. By the yells and vociferation exchanged from ship to
ship over the heads of the men under hatches, they were being
told to piss off—a response that Antonio cowered to hear. He
was quite right; the next sample of dialogue was three or four
cannon shot from the intruder, 'which putt this ex^{ate} and his
company in fear.' On top of this came the onrush and trampling
of continued assault—a boatload of new arrivals forcing their
way on board after a manoeuvre which sounds uncommonly like
ramming, though the men under hatches felt rather than saw it.

He adds that some men from the smaller depredator were kept prisoners by the men from the bigger one, which ends Antonio's testimony.

The pilot of the *St Anthony* however, Clement Moxiner, takes up the tale (by interpreter) at the point where the second load of men fought their way aboard. 'By force they entered and putt men in the ship. What otherwise passed between them he knoweth not,' he admits prudently, 'for that he was under hould, and left them to fighte it out.' But he can supplement this later. 'Savinge that when their fury was past and he was suffered to come upp, he saw two or thre of the lesser ship's company, and one of the bigger ship's, wounded and hurte.' Then he reverts to his gnawing professional grievance, still taking it as hard as the master. 'He and his company would have fought it out with the lesser ship before they yelded, ffor that the lesser ship was not of strength sufficient to have taken him', but the big parasite hovering on the outskirts spoiled everything. Also for the first time he describes the bigger ship: 'She was of the burthen of one hundreth tonnes, well armed and manned with aboute fiftye men.'

On Interrogatory he repeats the detail that on the big ship's assault 'there was fightinge with swords and great stirrings, and afterwards he saw fower of them wounded', and answers the question: Could he not have saved his ship by steering for the coast and beaching it? He could not, says Clement decisively; 'there was noe harbor nere, or place to run the shipp a grounde, for all that quoast [coast] was rockes'. He continues to sound hurt and downcast for not being able to save his ship.

After this, the questioning of others of the *St Anthony*'s company yields only one uncertain fact: Tomas Peires thinks that the master of the greater ship was named Paulo. Beside this there is apparently no identification, for all the pertinacity of the questioning, the same steely intention to get at the truth, by all and any means.

LICE AND NOTHING ELSE

The lethal consequences of a pirate attack, the loss of cargo, the possible injuries in fighting, the wounds and infections untended for lack of doctors, must be constantly present in the

mind of anyone reading such material, even if unconsciously.
Yet these horrid miseries are so seldom expressed in testimony
by word of mouth, that the experience of 'Christopherus
Cornelison of midleburgh', here offered, seems to include an
extra degree of eloquence as well as pain.

He was owner of the *St Mary* which carried goods of his own
and also goods of consignors; she was of 180 tons burden 'and
had a new gallery [sic] and was painted red besides, and had a
new foremast and a new bowspritte in her, and two overloppes'
[orlops]. With all this spruce and trim new dress 'she carried in
her XXVI great chests of suger, one hundreth and twenty
kintalls of brasill woode' and one unusual item: 'a pipe and a
haulfe of St Tomas sugar, *for the accompte of the poore of Zeeland.*'
Whether this was Christopher's personal charity or someone
else's is never explained, but one would like to think it Christopher's own. Whether or no, before sailing he made a deal
with a friend in Middleburgh, one Otto Vogle—'of good
credit and ability, and greatly employed in factoridge' whose
reputation, evidently, extended far beyond his home town.
Christopher's arrangement with him was this: if he ran into
complications of any sort, anywhere, he was to represent Otto
(for a consideration) as being owner of the *St Mary*, and this
would probably get him out of trouble. A good thing that he
arranged this, as it turned out.

The *St Mary* was bound for Venice; her first port of call was
in Portugal. Here Christopher was in hot water immediately.
'There was a generall imbargo of all hollanders goodes. And
this ex^ate was taken and putt in prison, and threatened to be
putt in the galleys, and that his shipp and goodes should be
confiscated.' In this desperate situation 'he was enforced to use
the meanes aforesaid'—attributing the *St Mary*'s ownership to
Vogle—and just as he had anticipated the magic name procured
his release, and he was allowed to resume his voyage. If he
did this with a relieved and happy heart, he was happy too
soon.

'On the Vth of December last (16?), nere Cape St Vincent,
the *Philip* (English) did sett uppon and take this ex^ate and his
said shipp. And took ye ex^ate and his purser into the *Philip*;
where the ex^ate was stripped and searched to his skin. And that
nighte X or XII of his men were stripped naked on borde the

St Mary and pushed into pinnaces while their blood sprung oute.' Evidently the *Philip*'s crew had searched the *St Mary* for valuables and had turned up nothing that they wanted; with stripping and wounding and shoving them naked into small boats they hoped 'to cause them to confesse where every pearle, every jewell and money were stored; as they who were soe tormented, told this ex^{ate}.'

Now—again—that full stop of indecision that follows so many piracies; those responsible have begun, tardily, to consider their own position before the law. In the present case the *Philip* most certainly did not have either a Commission to capture nor Letters of Reprisal; neither of which is mentioned from first to last. First of all her captain, in a belated gesture of legality, 'sente the *St Mary* with her lading to England'; then, seeing that he had aboard a number of the *St Mary*'s men, whom he had kept as prisoners, he sat down to consider (more and more uneasily, it seems) what to do with them. Meanwhile his crew, after the classic pattern—first the capture, then the carouse— had become so unmanageable that his decisions were delayed, and undoubtedly he was joining in the fun himself. This period of debate and indecision went on beyond belief; Christopher 'was kepte in the *Philip* about XXX dayes' before 'he was tould, by some of the seamen who spoke duch, that the captain mente to carry them to Barbary and there sell them for slaves.'

This horrifying intelligence with its attendant fear of 'the harde and cruell usadge of the turks' should have paralysed the English; instead, it seemed to have run their alertness up to fever pitch, or their desperation perhaps. Whichever it was, 'they watched for opportunity to escape', Christopher tells, 'and when he saw them of the *Philip* carlesse and making merry, he and thre more of his company did leape into a boate and cut the rope and rowed away to Sardinia, being the nexte [nearest] lande. And there they stayed for fyve weeks before they could get passage.'

How did they pay for passage, not having a penny among them? Almost undoubtedly it was Christopher, the merchant of standing, who secured them some little help. But if he got them passage in a ship, he could get them nothing else; without food, without bedding, sitting or sleeping on deck, transferring from ship to ship as chance would have it, 'they were caried to a place called San Tropez, then into ffrance, and from Ruane [Rouen] they came to Deepe [Dieppe], and from there to London.'

After Christopher the purser of the *St Mary*, Reiner Peterson, extends the testimony on cargo, giving it almost grain by grain of sugar. More importantly he names a second ship that took part in the piracy—the *Reprisal*—and has even found out some identities: the owner of the *Reprisal* is Sir John Gilbert, and Henry Carle is captain of the *Philip*. Reiner also mentions the stealing of £37 Spanish money, as well as the master's remarkably luxurious wardrobe: '2 new clokes, four surcoates, fyve vestes, goode store of linien, handkerchiefs and under breches'. This last item is surprising; 1600 is a very early date for under-drawers, male or female. Also Reiner makes the first mention, in the cargo, of an expensive article: 'There was a hundred onces [ounces] of muske in the cabon: and afterwardes he sawe pte of the said muske in the hands of Captain Croker of the *Reprisall*, and some of his company offered codes [cods: small bags] of muske to sell.' Incidentally he gives light on a shipper's method of pay: '[Cornelison] gave his mariners their wages from tyme to tyme when he made bargaines with the merchants; as the custome is amongst most shippers that goe on longe viadges.'

It is Christopher who describes his plight when at last he got to London. 'He brought with him lice, ragged apparell and lean cheekes, and nothing else; for he and his mariners begged all the way.' As for his presence at these Examinations: 'He came of him selfe to speke for his shipp and goodes, not being sente for by any.' He is there solely for revenge, and who can blame him?

It is Reiner, once more, who stamps Christopher with a seal final and beyond doubt: 'He knoweth that the shipps owner gathered some money during the viadge, for the use of the poore of Zeelande.'

A good man, Christopher, as well as a good employer; one hopes that his vile experience remained his only one.

SUMPTUOUS HAULS

This first glittering affair pleases not only by its distance from utilities like dried fish and wheat, but by its dancing reflection of fashion and the gay world. We need not speculate on the intensity of this perennial craze, in all ages and among all peoples, for jewellery. Without touching on royal ownership of ropes of enormous pearls both black and white and single stones of great size, everyone (almost literally) who could afford jewellery, did so. No noble has been painted who did not sport impressive necklaces, rings and earrings, to say nothing of garments so bedecked; Sir Walter Raleigh and Sir Christopher Hatton wear cloaks sewn with pearls at close intervals, while in any luxury cargo were always quantities of unset small pearls used for trimming. At court especially an unsuspected close watch was kept on anyone in attendance on royals, even distant attendance. Like the young lady who, being warned that her girdle possessed an insufficient number of pearls, passed this along—to mamma, naturally—who with great (money) difficulty scraped up another hundred pearls and sent them along. Ambassadors as well brought with them absolute jewellery shops to judge by the number of gold chains, plain or gemmed, that they handed out right and left as gifts.

One ship robbed was the *Cimba*; the pirates accused, Thomas Waighte and others, pleaded (surprisingly) not guilty. Here are the results of the examination:

2070	pearles, value	£80
3	ounces of pearls	15
2	strings of pearls	13
3	bunches of pearls	4
2	single pearls	20
2	pearls	20 solidem
		(gold pieces)
	garnets set in gold	30
1	ruby	(not valued)
1	polished diamond	40
50	silver pomanders	35
		£237

This brilliant assortment was accompanied by a few brilliant garments:

1	kirtle of velvet	£3
1	kirtle tufted with taffeta	10 gold pieces
1	lady's toga in silver brocade	(not valued)

The first warrant is marked *Billa Vera* (True Bill) which means that the accusation has stood proven up to that point: it seems reasonable what to expect for the pirates, especially if there were merchants in the jury.

'John Harper and William Deveninge of Dartmouth (and two others) on the 19th of August 1604, uppon a ffrench ffliboate, the *St Paule* of Talene, nere Malta in the Mediterranean Sea: did comit theft and spoyl by force of arms, viz, swords, daggers, knives, spears and bombards [these were real professionals, well equipped], did invade, break in and enter forcibly':

This opens another case of big-time piracy. Not in terms of money, but of high grade household valuables in such profusion as to give a run-down, complete almost, of the luxury trades then in existence. Indulgence is begged for the length of the list; after cargoes of wheat, timber and iron bolts this hoard is too delicious to omit. All values are in English money.

Muscadells laded at Venice	(value not given)
One butt [unam buttam] of sweet wine called Malmsey	XIII
20 quantities [sic] of English Arras	CI
20 carpets	XX
Bed furnishings of damask (all at once in English)	(value not given)
A bedd hanginge of crymson and white damask	X
A bedd hanginge of turkyshe cloth, quatuor liberaru in said monetas [sic]	IV
Bedd hangings striped in gold	XII
Taffeta striped in gold	XII
A damascene garment lined w. catskin	XX
A striped garment lined w. rabbit skin	X
A taffeta garment lined w. squirrel	XIII
120 handkerchiefs	5
6 silke quiltes	XII
50 napkins of linien	XIII
4 tablets [pictures?] of ebony, made in the image of Christ	XX
2 diamonds	LX
2 gold chaines	XX

A paire of bracelets	XV
One ruby	XXX
A paire of beades of Agathe [agate] with paternosters in gold	X

£449

The document is endorsed at the bottom: 'Sentenced by the Court and hanged March 30' (illeg.) Serve the lot of them right. It is improbable that any of the expensive loot was ever recovered.

Piracy done by the *Tilbury Hope* 'uppon a littel Duch shipp a hoy or wherye' (unnamed) gave an unexpectedly rich yield for the size of the victim, except—of all the imbecility—that it was committed in the Thames itself (super riviam Thamesas). The depredators were also accused of 'ill treting the pilot and the mʳ who, despairing of their lives', gave up the cargo of

A bason and euer (ewer) of silver	£XIII	VIs
12 silver vessells	XIII	
3 littel packets of silver (unworked?)	VIII	
{ 3 cloth packets embroidered in English, *The Liverie Companie*	XX	
2 silver candelabra	IV	
XI silver plates	X	
2 ,, saucers	X	
silver salt cellars	X	
2 gold bracelets	VIII	
1 kirtle of wrought velvet	V	
1 Crimson Damaske petticoat	VI	
Money stolen	VII	

£80

'Of which chattels,' the warrant continues, 'these [named] were founde in possession', and adds the sequel: 'William Jones, Thomas Paule, John Custer and Thomas Browne were hanged at Wappinge, XXV May 1604.'

The hoy sounds as if it were constantly engaged by silver-smiths, high-class tailors and embroiderers in Holland, and by gold- and silversmiths, tailors and jewellers in England.

*

More cargoes of enormous value might be quickly mentioned: the *George** robbed by Dutch pirates (1612) of a total estimated at '9098 ducketts, as by the scedle [schedule] may appeare: 20 canes [sic] of tawny velvet, 50 canes of black wrought rich taffeta, VIII canes of crimson damask, 5 iewells valew'd at 320 ducketts', and so it goes on, interminably and depressingly. Worse still is the pirates' treatment of 'the mᵣˢ boye; they tortured him with a corde walled [sic] about his heade until it brake, stabbed him in 4 or 5 places, and spoyled all that he had in shirtes, linnon and a hatchett, to the valew of VI or VII 1.' For this sort of gross inhumanity the Dutch were noted. But perhaps the top exhibit—as regards value—was the *Pearl* (4 April 1637). 'I have examined various persons,' says Justice Henry Martin, 'and uppon perusal of their examinations doe find' that the loss is a terrific one. £10,861.3 'and nyne pence'. Part of the cargo belonged to 'Sarah Weston widdowe, Abigail Leash, and other London/m'chants.' One or two items of loss are curious: '421 1 lent oute of the shipp; 845 1, other monies lent.' Was the *Pearl* a marine bank? a floating money lender?

By way of a final contrast—from the palace to the gutter—we might glance quickly at a humble cargo, our humblest so far to suffer piracy. Those arraigned are 'Nicholas Vaack mᵣ, Richard Harris mᵣˢ mate, one Stych mᵣˢ mate, Robert Phelips gonner'. Their ship was the *Rebecca* of London, which 'escried a Saile and gave chase thereto; and coming upp founde she was a Carvele of Sevill, laden with yearthen dishes'. This might have discouraged men of a loftier calibre: the *Rebecca*, nothing daunted, searched the caravel and turned up items slightly more marketable: 'two hundreth and twenty iarrs (jars) of oile, fourscore of Spanishe lamce (lamps), 16 Spanishe saddles, 30 iarrs of olives, and some cables'.

While this exploration was progressing, the second ship '*ffortune*—which had been two or thre leagues off'—came up and demanded her share of the loot. This was granted in the friendliest manner, and the goods were divided; possibly such a cargo was not worth fighting over. The slip-up in this heavenly concord came not from any dissension over cargo, but from the

* HCA 13–42—p. 65

caravel's passengers, of whom she carried two; one of them is present, burning to testify.

'We took all from the Carvel as lawfull prize,' Vaack concludes his testimony. Then on a dying fall he adds, 'Savinge only the yearthern dishes.'

IV
Piracy and Murder

'A pirate shipp *Sweepstake* attacked a ffrench shipp called the *Jaques de Octe* on 30 January 1560, the second yeare of the raigne of Queene Elizabeth. The pirates Norman Gascon and Acquitan Classisq, guilty of felonies, robberies, murders, illicit extortions and lamentable conspiracies are hereby handed over to the Marshalsea for safe custody, under strong and strict imprisonment, until you will carry out the sentence passed uppon them at Southwarke, in the accustomed place, on Monday 3rd of the present moneth of October [year illegible] about the seventh hower before noone.'

From this cheerless rendezvous at five in the morning we pass to a later document which again is not a warrant of execution, though the event is certain enough. '(1579) Johannes Gryffyn piratt, Robertus Lewis piratt and William Clerk piratt [are condemned] to a public death, and to your custody the said piratts are comitted.'

A slight step of six years supplies us (1585) with Thomas Seale and others in the *Jonas*, 'who attacked an unknown ship atrociously and cruelly [atrociter et crudeliter] and the said unknown ship did damage with bombards, falcons and minions. And with their swords did pierce [percusserunt] with lethal wounds [letalia vulnera] the bodies of certain unknown men, of which lethal wounds the said unknown men instantly died and gave up their lives.' Thomas and associates surface next in July 1586 when they come up for trial; this time the indictment specifies 'for spolinge and caringe away a ffrench shipp unknowne, with her lading of whyte wines'. By this time Thomas himself has confessed that some of the French ship's crew 'weare slaine in fights'. Eight days later (14 July) Thomas is handed over to the Marshalsea in the usual terms: strict detention till the date of execution 'for piratical felonies, robberies and murders': fairly quick work.

An example of 1605 is more interesting in that the warrant of

execution covers three murder trials held in succession on the
same afternoon. First we have the indictment of Thomas
Lawrence 'that at Southwarke on May 23 1604, for murdering
Andrewe ffurnace of the *Susan* of Wells, with a shott; p'ved by
the oath of Jo. Grewe mchant. And Robert Jones for murdering
William Andrews on bord the *Hopewell* in the River of Thames.'
Next is a mere scrap of document, which however fragmentary
—seven lines in Latin—makes an end of two of the foregoing:
'Thomas Lawrence est culpabilis murdri Andrewe ffurnace;
Robertus Jones est culpablis murdi William Andrewes.'*

With the third example† of the three however—'John Longe
et Daniell Cox for killing of Jaques ffaveras'—we have something more interesting not only as fact constantly enlarging,
but as legitimate ground for conjecture. (This case was begun
under Elizabeth I and finished under James I.) 'John Longe of
Arundel, for piracy and malefactions,' begins the indictment, 'on
the 17 November 1604; in the shipps the *Thomasine* and the
Talbott alias the *Dolphin*, nere the island of Sardinia, instigated
and seduced by devilish malice [instigaces diabolico et seducti
malitia], by force of arms, viz. swords, bombards, knives, spears
and shields, attacked a ffrench shipp called the *Serena* alias the
Mairmaid of Olona. And threw down and wounded Jaques
ffaveras, piercing him with lethal wounds, of which the
sd Jaques ffaveras did die, against the peace and dignity'
etc.

This, only the first shot in the locker, is succeeded by similar
deadly documents, some contributing new information. 'ffor
murdering Jaques ffavras [sic] alias James ffavras, on borde the
Serena,‡ runs another indictment, rather disturbingly, in view
of future disclosures. Both the accused have pleaded Not Guilty;
no witnesses are mentioned. In still another document the
condemnatory note becomes harsher and more implicit. 'John
Longe and Daniell Cox upon Jaques ffaveras did inflict a
deadly wound in his breast. Feloniously and maliciously,' it
continues, making things sure, 'a lethal injury, of which the sd
Jaques ffaveras suffered death.' A later mention of this killing is
dated,§ remarkably, 1607—Elizabeth has been dead three years
—when a quite big-time crook named John Exton (of whom

* HCA 1–5–39   † HCA 1–5–27
‡ HCA 1–5–38   § HCA 1–5–65

more later) unexpectedly enters the picture, accused of 'murthering of James ffaveras, trumpeter of the *Maremaid'*. Following this is a statement that 'Exton, by force of armes, did uppon the *Serena* comit piracies and felonies, and maltreat and menace those in her': but the next document, called an Inquiratur, gets down to the murder charge again without wasting time:* 'John Exton, diabolically instigated and seduced and of malice prepense, did lethally wound the aforesaid James ffaveras, of which the sd James ffaveras then and there did die. And of malice aforethought [precogitata] did do murder against the peace' etc., although the date of this, as mentioned, is 1607.

We are recalled to the trial of 1604, when Longe and Cox were sentenced for the murder of ffaveras. First of all the succession of documents it took to hang them suggests that the trumpeter must have been a general favourite for the legal process to have been pushed with such energy and pertinacity. But more alarmingly, in the trial of 1607, one John Guerin testifies, as an eye-witness, to Exton as the actual killer. Therefore, what of the two men executed in 1604 for the murder, after pleading Not Guilty? Were innocent men hanged? Or, if as undeniable pirates they were guilty—if not of one thing then another—yet we know that this carefree interpretation of responsibility was as abhorrent then to English law as it is now, and that a man gets it in the neck only for a criminal act he has, beyond all doubt, committed. All we know for sure is that the case is ended; from 1607, Faveras vanishes from the record.

By the way: the witness John Guerin comes briefly to life once more in a piracy case under Elizabeth I, though the law only caught up with them in 1606.† In this the pirates 'nere the isle of Sardinia, *and within the jurisdiction of the English Admiralty*, did menace Johannes Gueryn [sic] with threats of imminent death and apparatus of torment' [very unusual]. John's brother Martin Guerin was also aboard. They must have been prosperous merchants; a single item of their lading was 'one thousand and fifty quintals of iron, to the valew of one thousand good money'.

A warrant‡ that comes to grips with reality more quickly than the above series of trials is now disclosed to us, with a few moral flourishes added to boot: 'ffor singular felonies, murders,

* HCA 1–5–155   † HCA 1–5–111   ‡ HCA 1–5–119

homicide and piratical depredations, and for killing William
Pope a pilot, *and as a warning to others*: George ffaster, Edward
Mollett, George Humfrey' and three other men, are to be
'hanged at Wappinge around the nineth howr at dawn of day'—
and a curious view of nine in the morning. The writ is marked
with a note that execution has taken place; never did the good
folk of Wapping feed fuller on simple pleasures. A companion
writ* is unusually decorative, being written in a beautiful
script: one Richard Haydon is condemned for piracy 'to the
punishment of death' [penas mortis] but without specifying the
method. We are almost safe in assuming the gallows; when
worse than hanging was intended, the writ leaves us in no doubt
whatever. Richard is to be turned off 'apud Sefton on the 30th
day of August, in the yere 1605'.

Worse than hanging is illustrated in the next document:†
an enormous affair involving the trial of several men 'for thefts,
murders, felonies and homicides'. With these are included
extensive lists of jurors; moreover we must infer that these
juries were heavily involved not only among themselves but in
differences with the Judge, since the whereabouts of these rows
is plainly stated: 'in jures et tribunae sedentes'. After this
intriguing but undelineated warfare, one of the pirates is
sentenced to 'slow strangulation on the XXI day of March
1606'; two others are to be imprisoned, while three go free.
Evidently the jurors fought with the judge to some purpose.

From this dispute of tribunals it is almost a come-down to
mention again 'William Jones, Thomas Paule, John Custer and
Thomas Browne, hanged at Wappinge XXV May 1604',‡ but
an unusual circumstance entitles them to their share of immor-
tality. 'By muskett shott and by arrows they fell upon the *Susan*,
carrying out their injury by force and arms'. The owner (or
hirer) of the *Susan* was a woman, 'Audrey ffurnace of Lyme, to
whom they gave several lethal wounds, and who instantly died'.
Women merchants and factors were fairly numerous from much
earlier than James I, as any examination of the State Papers
Domestic can show; one is not sorry to see this lot of thugs get
their come-uppance for poor Audrey.

'All singular thefts, secret murders and homicides, spoils,
evil deeds [maleficia transgressiones] and other crimes, whether

* HCA 1–5–116   † HCA 1–5, p. 140   ‡ HCA 1–5–29

upon the high seas or the River Thames between the Bridge of London and the sea:

'Greeting: on the 26th day of March, at about the hour of dawn upon the same day, upon the proofs found by men of the burgh of Southwark and the Country of Surrey her towns and Hundreds, having lands, tenements to the value of 40 shillings, and possessions worth a hundred sterling :you shall inquire into the truth of all matter [presented], for our King and good Lord; who through us wills that justice be done.'

From Charles Earl of Effingham came countless summonses of a like nature, though one hopes they did not all call for immaculate dispensation of justice beginning at five on a March morning. These documents are under his seal (sub sigillo), a small ship in orange and brown wax with rigging exquisitely articulated; all these have vanished but this one happy exception fastened to a ribbon-like strip of parchment; an absolutely perfect seal which passes its life in a separate paper envelope. The writ mentions the Marshalsea (Marescaltus) as the official place of detention.

The following note of farewell might be regarded as a postscript to executions generally. In this case, the remains referred to are presumably of offenders more eminent than pirates; nevertheless all of them—whether quartered for treason or dropping to bits on the unfashionable Southwark gallows—share the common bond of nature so pitilessly evoked:

'As the gates of London are full of quarters not yet consumed [birds and decay combined] the heads [only] of prisoners will be set up, and the bodies buried'. *

Then follows a sort of disclaimer, gentle and apologetic: 'This order can be changed, if not liked.'

* CSPD, Vol. XXII, p. 334, No. 764

V
Suspensus erat

For the termination of Admiralty piratical cases—whether of execution, public whipping, imprisonment or otherwise—we have been left certain guide-posts, which are still not absolutely definite. Almost every juratorial script is labelled on the back, *Billa Vera*. Yet this does not indicate a decisive verdict; it only seems to mean that the accused have not yet succeeded in rebutting the items of accusation. The reader may conclude that this label is a strong indication that those on trial are well on their way to a sticky end—but not by any means, not with absolute certainty; a number of documents exist proving that men who certainly and technically deserved the worst were treated with remarkable clemency and got off scot-free.

In the trial of Charles Kettelly* for instance (1606) he is described at length as a pirate guilty of offences and spoils, yet on the reverse of the page is a reference to the 'sufficient services' of the man, followed by an indication (at least) of his pardon: 'it leafeth [leaveth] yt, your highnes, of y^r most abundant grace and goodness to graunt y^r most gratious lines of Pardon in due fforme, to be made and sente to the Tower, [date illegible] hereafter ensuing'. This pardon came from Prince Henry, James I's remarkable eldest son. It is reasonable to think that his great friend, then imprisoned in the Tower of London, put him up to it; Raleigh, after years of illicit dealing with pirates, knew of their secret valuable qualities. In any case this document is followed in short order by another: 'Pardon and remission are conceded, grace is looked upon favourably, by singular indications, for the benefit of the aforesaid Charles Kettelly. By statute and by act of evidence without restriction, they indicate the said Kettelly (is to go free) as in an act of p'liament, Edward III King of England; the which you have sustained.'

Kettelly was not the only one who cheated the hangman.

* HCA 1–5–94

'James by the grace of God etc.* As Robert Jones saylor on March 1, in the 4th year of the reign of Queen Elizabeth our sister and predecessor, by force and arms upon William Anderson of the ship the *Hopewell* within the jurisdiction of the Admiralty, did with a knife value fourpence, stab the sd William Anderson and give him a mortal wound [plagam mortalem] of the depth of four fingers and width of two fingers, of which the sd William Anderson did die.'

At this point, primed for Robert's hanging or worse, we receive a slight shock: 'We pardon, remit and relieve the sd Robert Jones of the pains of death; and those attaints, imprisonments, pains and penalties which the sd Robert has undergone, we do restore, by the authority of the Court of Admiralty, and by the ample grace of kingly power. And by good and sufficient security found by the sd Robert, binding upon his heirs and successors, form and effect are hereby given to this our act.' Less favourable is the next exhibit,† from James 'to his beloved and faithful Julius Caesar, salute: As we by our good authority have commiserated and eased John Jennings and William Curtis of their imprisonment for their sd offences of spoil of piracy, attested by judicial proceedings, we specify thus: the said persons having found sufficient security by act of p'liament of Edward III, and also by our act, shall be entitled to bail as a relief from their servitude, six bailors [manucaptori] being sufficient security, for a period of six months.' Whether John and William got off entirely in the end, is uncertain.

The next candidate was unreservedly lucky: ‡ Morgan Brooke robbed a Spanish ship of its cargo of quality foods—'large jars of delicacies, apparatus and appendages [apparatiis et accessiones] of wine making'—but the verdict on the reverse of the document is *Ignoramus*. By the way, one Peter Christmas, pirate, is also released on bail; could he have been an ancestor of the great marine carvers, Garrard, John and Matthias? Christmas is a very uncommon surname.

If the expression *Ignoramus* has appeared on hundreds of documents seen by one researcher, it must appear (literally) on tens of thousands. Sometimes, out of a number of accused, the juries would make a single exception: out of the trial of eight

* HCA 1–5–101   † HCA 1–5–98   ‡ HCA 1–5–121

pirates, against the name of one man is marked *Ignoramus*;* again, in the trial of the pirate crew of an unnamed ship which 'in the Road of Saphia, aided and abetted [auxiliate sunt et abbettarunt] other pirate ships', Hugo Robinson's name alone is followed by *Ignoramus*. Making distinctions of this sort, out of whole crews of accused, indicates rigid attention on the part of the jury, also highly individual viewpoints. A still stronger testimony of their unsparing hard work is the following exception, after sitting on a number of pirates:† 'We have examined personally Richard ffisher of Redruth in Surrey, and with all humility present and exhibit the said short judgment of pardoning him by commission of the seal of England: by reason that it has been shown that the offence is lightened and forgiven.' No fuller explanation follows, but it seems that Richard has a good chance of getting away with it.

Quite different, but with its own slight shock value, is the indictment of Arthur Chambers.‡ In sonorous Latin it goes on and on rigorously and harshly for two full quarto pages that one waits, with entire confidence, for the death sentence. Instead, without preparation, the document announces, 'We pardon, remit and release the sd Arthur Chambers from the said indictment and punishment of death [perdonamus, remittimus et relaxavimus prefati Arthur Chambers de penas mortis].' If the rest of the judgment were not lost, we might have some slight indication why. In the case of small piracies it seems that the verdicts tended to let the malefactors off easily:§ various men in 'a shipp called a whereye, did rob a small German shipp name unknown called a Crayer, on the high seas near Margate' [navicula vocata a Crayer sub alto mari impta Margatt]. The values in this robbery are all expressed in *solidarum* (shillings) rather than pounds. Another example is of mere sneak thievery: Thomas Driver and another name (struck out) 'in a boate, in the night time, in the River Thames opposite Wappinge, did stele from the *Providence* a cable and a semi-cable [cabulam et semi-cabulam] worth VI.XIII.O.' The thieves are described as sailors and watermen, undoubtedly a tough lot. Both indictments, and similar ones, are inscribed *Ignoramus*.

Another road of escape from the gallows or other punishment

---

was the ability to pay counsel. In citing one such example in defence of a really bad egg named Fenner, we might remember that the indictment against him included not only repeated piracy with violence, but also a charge of murder. The following quotation is partial: the crimes date back to 1598.*

(January 1606) 'Exceptions to two Indictments of piracy against William Fenner, gent: First the indictment doth not say *piratice et felonice* [piratically and feloniously] for each word is necessary in such a judgment . . . Thirdly, the Judgment "that Thomas Rogeret was pierced by a leaden bullet in his body, by which he was lethally wounded and died": This is very insufficient, for it is not expressed upon what parte of his body was the Stroke and Wounde: and what was the profundity or Latitude of the Wounde. Also there needeth not any profundity or Latitude to be shewne, except it is to be shewne what parte of the body it has penetrated. And therefore the Judgment is insufficient' etc.

Whether these delicate distinctions and refinements would have pleased poor dead Thomas we do not know, but they produced two postscripts below the final paragraph: 'I thinke these indictments are insufficient for these Causes, and the exceptions make the indictment void.' (Signed, Richard Stention). 'ffor this and others, what cause we ar [sic] of the same opinion.' (Signature illegible.)

Having scoured over, briefly, that array of formal documents which mostly fail to guarantee execution or no execution we land, and high time too, on the ground of incontrovertible evidence. These particular testimonies are written at the bottom of a *Billa Vera*, and almost always in the same formula: *Suspensus erat*. Since Wapping appears to have been particularly favoured as a turning-off place, *Suspensus erat* will be often followed by *apud Wappinge*, or in less frequent cases by *apud Southewarke*; we also have one *apud Sefton* (illegible).

In a good many verdicts of death, the charge of piracy is joined to the charge of murder. Not in every instance, however; one hesitates, in this long-gone trouble and murkiness, to draw conclusions. Edward Hall† for instance, curiously defined in the

---

* HCA 1–5—pp. 86–8, 90–2   † HCA 1–5—(unnumbered)

indictment as 'a London merchaunte' is charged only with straight piracy and no mention of bodily harm unless we accept the qualifying 'violently', but on the bottom of the parchment we find in tiny, almost invisible letters, 'Suspensus erat dictus Edwardus Hall XXV May 1604.' Not many condemned were honoured, in this formula, by an inclusion of their names. Edward must have had means; it took *six* True Bills in parchment (some of them large and handsome) to do him in.

For John Sallowes, one Allyn and others, however, it took only four True Bills. Their crime, beside piracy on the *Speedwell* of London, was plain ordinary murder 'upon the pilot and the master, who had resisted them bravely with muskets and arrows, and whom for this they killed.' The hangings are certified by 'Suspensus erat [bad grammar] John Sallowes et Allyn at Wappinge, XXI April 1604.' After this an unusual note: 'Richard Gaile, twice interrogated by the Spanish Legate, was reprieved by the king'; no further explanation is given. Each of the four True Bills, to dispel any doubt at all, is marked *Suspensus erat*.

The hangings of four men for piracy on 'a ffrench ffliboate'* and of four others,† is distinguished mainly by the richness of the cargo in both cases. The first lot receive the unsuitable note, Suspensus, and the second assortment are more handsomely treated, in point of grammar at least: 'Suspensi erant apud Wappinge XXV May 1604.' On this same date, by the way, we note two other hangings‡ for men indicted in the Faveras murder; the 25th was another gay day for Wapping. The hundreds and hundreds of piracies on the Thames itself are usually petty affairs but the case against 'Robertus Harrod de Rye' and at least six others, is much more sinister.§ These again were, apparently, all watermen, who did 'theft and spoil upon a French ship called *The Flower of Luce*, and did curse and insult the pilot and master and other persons of the sd ship, until they despaired of their lives'. The *Flower* was a bad investment from start to finish; all they got for their trouble was a little taffeta (unam packetam continentem peciam tufted Taffeta'). The sentence, badly begrimed and almost illegible, seems unique of its kind: 'Hanged in the vaults, Robertus Harrod, 21 April 1604;

---

* HCA 1–5–26   † HCA 1–5–28
‡ HCA 1–5–27   § HCA 1–5–24

and Robertus Jones alias Commer, a gunner, 25th of May following.' The location of 'the vaults' is never given.

Aside from the ordinary dangers of being a pirate there were other risks of the trade, such as an indiscreet choice of the ship to be attacked.* On 14 December 1604, 'on the sea near the Islands of Bayon [Bayonne] five marauders attacked the Portuguese ship called *Our Lady of the Conception*'. So far so good, except that 'the Portuguese are in firm peace, federation and friendship with our King, and subjects of Prince Phillipp the Spanish King'. Also, beside the valuable cargo of timber and sacks of hides, the pirates took 'an Alexandrian travelling carriage belonging to [illeg.] Gonsalvo'—who might have been anyone of consequence from an ambassador downward. The mixed verdict on this is interesting. Above two names, one of which is John Jennings, are the words *non cul pose ca vul* (not guilty so far as the wounding is concerned). Yet in the end we find, 'Jennings, Curtys and Carbyn were hanged'. The place of execution is given as Wapping, but no date.

The next case† is a different matter altogether, the mere mass of documentation being terrifying, and also—most unusually— with lists of jurors mixed in. This is the trial referred to previously, in which the arguments among the jurors them- selves, and their disagreements with the judge, are cited time and again. The charges against several men, the usual 'thefts, murders, felonies and homicides' must have been of an unusual atrocity to promote such wrangling; it is our loss not to be able to recreate the voices, juridical and judicial both. In the end, one pirate (name illegible) is sentenced to 'slow strangulation at Southwarke on the XXI day of March 1606', an unusual sentence in these papers so far, even perhaps unique. Two other men, Richard Trevor and John Pope, get prison sentences. Again unusual; where murder is concerned there seems no halfway house, the guilty are hanged and the not guilty go free. Pirates in prison are almost always waiting for trial, or found guilty and waiting for execution.

As to confessions: in almost every case among these thou- sands, some of the pirates admitted some or all of the alle- gations; others did not; still others refused to plead either guilty or not guilty, a course of action carrying its own special

---

* HCA 1–5–80   † HCA 1–5—(no number)

penalty, to be discussed later. As for the pirates who admitted the charge: did this act of confession shield them, in any degree at all, from the death sentence? The trial of 'piratts arraigned at Southwarke on 16 February 1607* mentions their pillaging of four ships—of which one, beside her lading of 'clothe of gould, clothe of silver, damasks and taffetas' carried '2500 paire of silke stockings'. Cleanliness was not the only thing Elizabeth made fashionable in England. Only one man, Gerrard Scottle, 'confessed; denied by the rest'. After this one looks, with reasonable confidence, for Gerrard's acquittal or at least a modified punishment, but not at all: 'Garret [sic] Scottle de Ratcliffe, condemnatus erat et consideratu per curiam [judged by the Court] ut esset suspensus.'

As the lax and slovenly Jacobean reign progresses, and pressure on the Court of Admiralty becomes more and more severe, we find astonishing numbers of pirates coming up for trial at once, and the thought of the Examinations that preceded those occasions makes the heart quail. In the pirates arraigned at Southwark on Saturday 22 October 1609, we have —in succession—groupings of twelve, thirteen and twelve again, thirty-seven in all; the document intones over and over, *they are indicted*; no absolute guide without *suspensus*, but it sounds like the high jump for the lot. On 1 September 1608 we have judgments on seventy pirates in groups of seven or eight; on a last remaining fragment (no date) Richard Cole and Thomas ffreeman are sentenced to the Marshalsea, and after that are to be hanged at Wapping. For William Pope, a sentence to the Marshalsea only, again unusual.

As time marches on, evidences of execution are somewhat different in form, name and source. 'Hec [hic] Indentura† made on the Sabbath day [Court business was evidently still done on Sundays] 3rd day of October 1610, between his Majesty King James and William Robinson, custodian mariscalte': four names follow, 'sentenced to death at Southwarke [convictorum morti apud Southwarke]: this leaves us in no doubt. Neither does the case of the '*Black Horse* of ffleming,' 1607, robbed by several including Richard Sherlock and William Campion (celebrated name) of cloths and silks to the value of £275, and £23

* HCA 1–5–194, 200   † HCA 1–6—pp. 181, 249

English. All are condemned except one man, against whose name we find, 'Ignoramus quo ad William Campion'. A certain mild pleasure at seeing anyone called Campion get off is quickly checked a long way further on, nine years later in fact: Thomas Campion is arraigned (1616)for various piratical and evil deeds'. This is marked True Bill, so they have him dead to rights so far. Could the two be brothers? Or is this an independent Campion, all on his own? A feverish hunt for the relationship, or for anything more on Thomas, yields nothing whatever.

Another Thomas* has a good run for his money, and a providential release. This Thomas Tompkins, another big-time pirate, comes up before the Court on four major counts, of which two are 'for killing and murdring of ffrancis pandalogo, m^r of the Venetian shipp the *Balbina*, and for killing another Venetian man unknowen: for taking of 233 peeces of brode clothe, 950 pound of cochanile, 10,000 yeards of sattin and silkes; for taking 100 bagges of cort [cord?], 75989 ducketts in money', and many other things of less value. Just as we are working up a lively desire to see Thomas get his come-uppance, comes the note: *Died in prison*. Eight names below attest the decease; rather disappointing. Looking further we find a slip of parchment with upper scalloped edges, and a parchment ribbon threaded along its bottom. This charming little affair, suggestive of an invitation to a children's party, informs us that 'this indenture between Thomas Ways, Custodian of the Marshalsea, (and other officers) acknowledges receipt of Thomas Sutton, condemned to death [morti adiudicae], and the execution to be done by one Jasper Swift.' This is the only mention of an executioner to be found in the documents examined. Jasper, plus the unusual prettiness of the indenture, makes two bonuses altogether, or ought one to say boni? This example is of Elizabeth's reign.

On 4 June, 1633,† Giles Pansfoote is in trouble, indicted for receiving from Henry Robinson, Samuel Sweetinge and John Twirle alias Toodle, 'one Agate Cupp like a small boke, sett in gould with forty thre pearles uppon it, garnished with divers little Stones, stolen from a ffrench barke called the *Magdalen* of Deepe' [Dieppe]. Also, from the same three lads, he has received 'a Silver Cupp, a Silver Salte Sellar and other peeces of

* HCA 1–6—p. 199   † HCA 1–7—No. 91

plate' stolen from the *Blessing* of Sandwich. All three pirates are
condemned to death, but opposite Giles's name is a curious
note, 'non cul nec augugit' (not guilty nor escaped; i.e.
attempted to escape?), which sounds equal to a release. He
must have proven himself a merchant who bought the silver
unknowing of its origin; this is a little difficult to swallow. A
separate allegation confirms that the three pirates 'are found
guilty modo et forma su', while an attached note contributes its
own pleasant little patch of fog: 'The Foreman and others of the
Jury said that he values the Chambers but at 2 £.'

We now have what seems to be a woman pirate, Elizabeth
Patrickson,* indicted with her husband for 'robbery, murder
and other maritime offenses'; on extended examination she
turns out to be more of a riverside thief, though undoubtedly an
ugly customer. 'William Patrickson and Elizabetha his wife, in
the Thames near the City bridge,' runs the first indictment, 'did
take one hundred pounds English money and various goods;
and upon Henrico Marten a Doctor of Law, did comit piracy,
robbery and murder, between the first and second hours on the
10th day of March 1634.'

The second presentment is badly damaged, but not less
ominous for that; in the third paragraph of this Elizabeth is
named with alarming conspicuousness, William not mentioned
at all except as her husband. She has been for an interval
(illegible) in 'his Maties Gaole of Newgate, for that she
confesseth [torn] till she shall speake . . .' [torn].

This almost invisible entry is no doubt important; the
reference to torture seems almost beyond doubt. '. . . faile you
not,' the presentment continues, 'as you will answere to the
contrary.'

A third indictment 10 March (1634)† confines itself to
William's thefts, so does a fourth; in neither of these is the
murder mentioned. A fifth indictment is only a list of pirates,
William's name among them, but in No. 6 indictment‡
Elizabeth comes into her own, though she has to wait till page
4 to do so. This page she occupies totally, albeit the charge of
murder again fails to appear. Her loot (in addition to joint

* HCA 1–7—pp. 109, 155, 161   † HCA 1–7—p. 155
‡ HCA 1–7—pp. 101/61

responsibility for her husband's massive thefts) has been in-
creased by 'one blacke Turkey gowne for a woman, water'd and
laced, with a blacke imbroyder'd Satten lace; one flaxen pillow
beere; one course [coarse] Towell, one greene Saye apron;
unam pugionem [one dagger]; one flaxen sheete', etc. After this,
again with menace, is noted *simile* (the like accusation), wife of
the aforesaid William, together with a second list of her swipes:
'unam mappam [one tablecloth], one grey clothe doublett' and
other things valued at £16.

What happened to William, and above all to Elizabeth? No
final reference to hanging seems to exist in either case. Yet in
Elizabeth's, the evidence of the second presentment seems to
put the matter beyond doubt. From 1604, torture was almost
invariably a prelude to death; exceptions are rare. William's
case, the rack excepted, must have been similarly punished. The
Court of Admiralty, one might think, would not be specially
inclined to lenience for the murderess of a Doctor of Laws. But
it took them six presentments before they could nail Elizabeth.

VI
Buggery

In 1797 St Vincent, one of the greatest of English admirals, sent to the Admiralty a routine report of the court-martial and execution of two homosexuals. This procedure illustrates for us the fact that by the above date such offences (if they can be so named) were now handled *in situ*, with judgment and verdict being delivered where the offence was committed. The seventeenth century, however, was different; by a fair amount of evidence, cases of buggery were confined to the Admiralty Court.

A first indictment,* dated 1 September 1608, is against 'William Audley, ffor comitting buggery with Arthur Jackson on borde the *Surety* on the high seas'. After this, a deadly admission: 'Confessed by him selfe and proven' by two talebearers. With that fatal 'confessed by him selfe', also with memories of St Vincent's merciless procedure, a desponding view of William's fate is inevitable—a view confirmed by another document (unnumbered) which opens ominously: 'The jurors, having inquired and considered the charge against William Audley, accused of that horrible sin and crime called in English buggery as it is alleged [pretenditur] with the sd Arthur Jackson in the *Surety*': after this moral blast, surely the worst is coming. Therefore, with an undeniable sense of anti-climax, we read the final verdict: 'We do not know, and therefore they are dismissed.' This seems remarkable after the man's own confession, but is perhaps another proof of the very frequent reasonableness—not to say the unexpected humanity—of Jacobean jurors.

The next example, far more extensive, is heralded by two writs of commitment,† almost copies of each other; both are addressed to (presumably) the head gaoler of the Marshalsea: '29 September 1634: To charge you to take into your Custody the body of Robert Hewitt Marriner, suspected to have

* HCA 1–5–223   † HCA 1–7–116, one unnumbered

comitted Buggery in the ship the *Mary*, and safely to keepe untill he shalbe Legally delivered.' (Signed) Henry Martin, Deputy. The second writ to the same address, labelled (unusually) *A Warrant of Comitment*, begins a shade more imperiously: 'To charge and comaunde you to take into y^r Custody', but otherwise follows the first word for word.

On the heels of the above prelude we come to our second example—not piratical, but of a massiveness most unusual. It consists of no less than three writs issued against the same offender and dated two years after the commitments—1636. The first of the series* opens: 'That Robert Hewitt with a boy, George Hungerforde, most criminally and feloniously, against nature, did comitt that crime detestable and abominable of Sodomy, in English of Buggerye, not to be named between men, against the peace' etc. Number two,† after a similar pious blast, again specifies Hewitt and another victim, Marmaduke Warnham (Marmaducum Warnham puerum masculum). The final writ‡ names the victim as Roger Head; the offence is the same. All this carry-on was in the *Royall Mary*, and apparently in the course of one single voyage; how did he think he was going to get away with it? But again the surprise lurks in ambush: all three writs, in spite of having True Bill written on the back, display over Hewitt's name, *Non cul*. 'No man's luck can go further,' as an eminent Victorian once said (in quite another context), and certainly this practitioner—found innocent not on one but on three counts—has had his share of luck. Somewhere in the papers from 1636 on we might find Hewitt in more trouble of the same kind, or even encounter him on the gallows. The one that we do find later on is Audley; the fact that this time the charge is of piracy seems to fade—by contrast with the earlier charge—into proper insignificance.

---

* HCA 1–5–53/120   † HCA 1–5–52/121   ‡ HCA 1–5—(unnumbered)

VII
Peine Forte et Dure

This horror, also called *Pena Fortis et Dura*, or (ungrammatically) *Poena Forte et Dure*, is the equivalent of 'pressed to death' in English. Not that English is often used, as if hiding behind Latin or French could mitigate, or a little conceal, what was being done. The writer believes that statements are not unknown, declaring this punishment a mere fiction. It was anything but a fiction; a number of writs carrying the sentence are in existence, of which one is an illustration in this book. It must be noted that the verdict of *Peine Forte* was exclusively inflicted—with one exception, which will be noted—on those who, refusing to plead either guilty or not guilty in Court, simply 'stood mute'. Perhaps the best that can be said in palliation of it is, that it was passed, undoubtedly, on men guilty of the most hideous barbarities—to say nothing of the piracy itself—and that they were simply getting what they had handed out, with a little extra piled on. No matter; it remains hard to swallow a measure so singularly Asiatic. The single stroke of the axe, the fifteen-minute agony of the rope, even the drawing and quartering of men still alive, cannot compare with this. Any attempt at description is happily obviated by the unsparing particularity and explicitness of the documents themselves.

(1604)* 'The said Philipus Warde stubbornly stood dumb [stet mutus] and sentence of death was passed on him, that he might have *peine forte et dure* on the next day, viz the 3rd of July, without the prison of Marshalsea, he should be pressed to death'.

We are thankful too soon that the above example, at least, spares us the details. Not so the next† (1605) in the name of Charles Lord Nottingham, who 'delivers over Williamus Harvye (Harvy, Harvie) for singular felonies, for murder and homicide of William Zouch, and for piratical depredations, the

* HCA 1–5–65   † HCA 1–5–74

said Williamus Harvye being now in the gaol of Marshalsea and detained at the king's pleasure, having to answer before a jury of his country. By which the said Williamus Harvye, at the ninth hour of the morning near the said prison of the Marshalsea, shall be thrown upon the ground and weighed down by stones over his body, all excepting his arms, so that he lies directly on his back. And make a hole in the ground beneath his head and put his head in the hole. And thus lying covered with stones and iron, while he lives he shall have of the coarsest bread and water. And if he eats he shall not drink, and if he drinks he shall not eat.' This writ of execution is the single one, previously referred to, which contains no mention at all of his having 'stood mute'.

The third specimen* catches up with Philip Ward, whom we have seen standing mute. 'For piratical depredations, spoil, rapine and murder of Nicho. Zouch (brother of William?) and William Pope, merchants: A hole shall be dug in which their [his and Harvye's] respective bodies shall lie naked and shall be weighed down with stones and iron as heavy as can be. And while they live they may have the worst bread and water of that prison, neither clean nor running. And on the day they drink they may not eat, and on the day they eat they may not drink.'

Here we beg indulgence for partially citing the original, since the English does not seem (to one person) to possess the bite and barbarity of the Latin:

'Nudos preter braccas suas super terram, Ac super dorso respectum directo, et foramen in terra sub eoro caput in eodam, tantum lapidibus et ferro quantum possunt, et quandum vivent habebunt de pane pessimo et aquam prisonae illi proprium non currenta sed slunto [?], et illa die qua comedent non libent, ac illa die qui libent, non comedent.'

Charles Earl of Nottingham has been mentioned as an especially savage pursuer of pirates; on any writ where his name occurs one is sure either of most sweeping edicts against them, or of equally ferocious sentences passed on the pirates themselves. In this particular specimen dated January 1605,† unusually lengthy of its kind, Teye Corbus and Richard Greenlese are indicted 'for murder and piracy, depredations and

* HCA 1–5–75   † HCA 1, Vol. 2, no. 85

other crimes.' In a succeeding document* Greenlese is condemned to that punishment'called in English, pressed to death (presso mori)'. On Corbus (a Swede) the sentence is milder, also a little unusual in this connection: 'he is to be beaten publicly, in the sight of flagellis publico in conspectu. . . .' (illeg.) Both men are mentioned, prior to the execution of sentences, as being in the Marshalsea.

In the shufflings and burrowings of any such hunt as this one, unexpected things may come to the top. One such item† is the sentence of *Peine Forte et Dure* inflicted—staggering thought—on a woman. This rare piece of grisliness does not come within Admiralty Court cases but is linked to them by what one might call land piracy, since the victim was an importer—in a fairly large way of business—who rented for his transactions and purchases a warehouse near the port. The first document is an indictment‡ against Thomas Keeler and Alice Keeler spinster (brother and sister apparently) 'who have in the night time robbed and feloniously burgled (burglarent: improvised verb) Henry Bartlett of six silver clocks value £50, 80 table napkins value £20, 2 tableclothes worth £20, one piece of linen cloth, one piece of woollen cloth, a wallet worth £12, one box of diett bread worth £6, 2 pieces of linen cloth called lawne, and other goods of the same Henry Bartlett, against the peace and dignity' etc.

The writ§ which discloses the outcome of the trial cites one Thomas Williams, an accomplice of the Keelers; he is not mentioned again. The document rehearses the list of stolen goods, and has a brief line at the end: 'Alice Keeler shall suffer *poena forte et dure*, and Thomas Keeler shall be hanged.' Therefore, even if the writ makes no mention of it, we know almost certainly that Alice was the tough one who refused to plead one way or the other; her brother was made of softer stuff. In the face of courage like hers—even senseless courage—one is left by no means admiring, only somewhat shaken.

---

* HCA 1, Vol. 2 (number illegible)
† Assizes: 35/59/6, nos. 24, 37. I owe this example to the kindness of Dr Cox, Round Room, PRO.
‡ (Ibid.) no. 24
§ (Ibid.) no. 37

VIII
A Horror Story

Atrocities of every kind, to person and property, are of course staple in any account of piracy. Yet, even in so brief and superficial a survey as this one, there occur episodes which—by some grotesque quality or dimension—seem to transcend the commonplace brutalities and enter into an unfamiliar realm of their own.

One such example is dated 22 June 1600,* and the person under examination is (unusually) one of several pirates from the same ship, by name Christopher Cornelison, who testifies through a translator. In retrospect, looking over his testimony, it is evident how desperately he is lying and evading. All of them were lying, with good reason; the thing does not show its face till the very end.

Christopher begins by not answering the first nine questions on grounds of ignorance. With the tenth he loosens up and begins the tale of his ship (*Philip*) accosting three ships at once —the *St Mary*, the *Admiral*, and the *Vice-Admiral*. The *Philip*, 'a shipp of warre and warlickly furnished', haled the *St Mary* and demanded in ffrench whom they were, whence they came and whither they were bounde; and she answered againe in ffrench' with the requisite information. The pirates put the same questions to the *Admiral*, which gave the same answers. 'Then the Captain of the *Philip* willed them to strike, and the *St Mary* did p'sently [immediately] strike.'

The *Admiral*, however, was of tougher grain. 'The ffrench men answered they would not strike; where upon the *Philip* shott at the sd *Admiral* thre or fower shotts and so leyde her on borde.' Now an unexpected setback for the pirates, in the very moment of victory. 'And as we were bordinge, one of the portes of the *Philip* was broken, and the *Philip* fell off againe.' Repair of any damage that could let in the sea was not to be postponed. At once the *Admiral*, not slow to take advantage of

* HCA 13–34

the mishap, 'sayled on her course, and the *Vice-Admiral* hoysed [hoisted] upp her top saile and followed after.'

Much good their flight did them; the broken port was instantly patched up and pursuit was resumed. 'The *Philip* shott at the *Admiral* both with greate ordinance and musketts; and both the ffrench shippes answered in like manner with greate and smale ordinance. And the *Philip* chardged againe the third tyme, and layde her aborde, and made a rope fast uppon the ffrench shipp.' Yet once more, to the apparent victors, another accident. 'The rope brake or slipped,' Cornelison pursues, 'and thereby the *Philip* fell off and drove uppon the other shipp the *Vice-Admiral*, beinge hard asterne.'

Now he is entering—and well he knows it—upon the dangerous ground.

'We entered our men into the same. And as some of the english men were takinge down the ffiagge, the ffrench men cried, What will you doe, what will you doe, the shippe doth sinke! Whereuppon the english men ran back and cast some hande gonnes [culverins] of the ffrench shipp into the *Philip* [stealing what they could] and left the ffrench shipp, and gott them selves into the *Philip* againe.'

At this point he veers off—deliberately, one feels—and offers some bloody but irrelevant details.

'He knoweth that in the sd fyghte, nyne or ten of the company of the *Philip* were wounded and slayne by shott that came from the ffrench shipp. Whereof the Captaine lost a legge, an other lost an arme, others were shott through and one of the *Philip*'s men was slayne; and one english man whom he saw cast overborde.'

From here on, again, he makes a valiant effort to detach himself completely from the main course of events.

'And when this ex^ate sawe all this, he feared there would be much trouble amongst the companye.'

In other words he began to think—unless he is lying completely, which is probable—of the consequences. In the thoughtful and meditative frame of mind which he has described, he withdrew modestly from the scene of combat.

'He wente under hould and stayed not above haulfe or quarter of an hower. And then, hearing no noice above he came upp on the decke and sawe but one of the ffrench shipps in syght. And asking for the other, the company reported she was sounke and gon. And looking oute he sawe some chistes and barrells, and some of the ffrench men swimminge and tumblinge in the sea. And he also sawe a boate putt furth with men in yt, who rowed towardes the sd men and goodes swimminge in the sea. *But whether yt were to save the men or the goodes, he knoweth not.* (Writer's italics.) But,' he half-contradicts himself, eager to put the blame on anyone else, 'the m^r of the *Philip* called unto them in the boate and comanded them to returne to the shipp, and saved not any of the sd ffrench men or the goodes, of this ex^{ates} certain knowledge.'

At this point the Interrogatory begins; judging by its result the questioning must have taken a new, sharp and formidable turn. A pity that we cannot supply it, nor (except in our own imaginations) the stringent voice of the examining Justice that was driving Christopher further and further into the damning truth. We might also remember that, for a witness too unsatisfactory or too stubborn, there lurked in the background another presence—the rack. Now, always sticking strenuously to his story of having gone below in the crucial half-hour or so, and of having had nothing to do with the tragedy, he unveils the final, terrible scene.

'By reporte of the marriners, some of the ffrench men, seinge their shipp sinkinge, gott on the bowe spritt which was over towarde the fore part ot the *Philip*, with intente to leape into the *Philip* and save their lifes. And holding upp their handes desired the english men to save their lifes, for godes cause. And the english men in the *Philip* threatened them with their pikes in their handes, that yf they offered to come into the *Philip* they would run them through with their pikes. And soe they all perished, as the marriners of the *Philip*, who sawe yt, tould this ex^{ate}. For this ex^{ate},' he reminds the Justice, for the tenth time, 'being under houlde, sawe not the same. And this ex^{ate} herde saye,' he adds, unweariedly upholding his distant rôle, 'there were XXIII p'sons in the said shipp which soncke, and were all lost in ye same.'

Christopher is not quite through; even after the revealed crime, he has another modest bombshell.

'He herde yt reported on borde the *Philip*, that Mr Drake was owner of the *Philip*.'

Does this last disclosure account for the veil that descends—
or seems to descend—on any further proceedings in the murder
of the *St Mary*'s entire crew? A trial may have been held,
sentences may have been imposed; some lucky researcher may
find them one day. In place of verdicts, however, we do have
some interesting if lesser facts. Christopher's long and ex-
hausting examination was preceded by similar examinations of
five of his shipmates; not one of them makes the faintest
reference to the fate—before their eyes—of the *St Mary*'s
company. They had more nerve than Christopher, or else more
luck—the luck being that the Justice, at the moment, happened
to begin examining the robbed survivors. One of these, the
purser, gives a poignant account of the *St Mary*'s lading, and
above all the lading of the bigger ship, the *Admiral*. The *St
Mary*'s cargo was not so impressive, consisting mainly of
'great chistes of sugar', yet sugar was commanding a high price
in Venice (her destination) though the purser cannot tell
exactly how great their loss was 'without his skedle and his
boke'; he puts it, tentatively, at £500—to say nothing of the
total loss of the ship herself, 'of one hundreth and eighty tonnes,
very well furnished, fitted and victualled, and worth not less
than eight hundreth pounds.'

On the *Admiral*'s pillage, he has a good deal more to say.
Her lading was so considerable that he had had an assistant 'to
helpe him make upp the reckoning', but even without his book
he indicates a heavy cargo. 'Sugers, brasil wood, and other
tymbers; a hundreth onces of muske, balm and parritch [sic].
Also he knoweth that the mr had XXVI l in Spanish money
stoured at his beds endse, for thi exate helped to tell [count] the
sd money and sawe it putt in a bagge.' He adds that the musk
(immensely valuable) was stored in the same place as the
money; that must have been an odoriferous bag of coins. In
some additional testimony Tyfe Barrenson, the *Philip*'s
carpenter, unveils a trifling difference of opinion between the
Philip's Captain Carle and himself: 'The Captaine chardged
him that he had sworne untrewly, and there uppon the sd
Carpenter drew his knife and cutt him in the face, for so
chardging him.'

But after the drowning of a shipload of men, little of all this
reaches us. Even some stray bits offered by Sebastian Baccaliere,

owner of lading in the *Admiral*—that he has heard that 'm^r Drake' and his partner Captain Jan Gilbert have disposed of 'the brasil woode and other tymber'—fail to make much impression. This is not the first time we have seen a great name lurking in the background of piracy; and if Sir Walter Raleigh, why not Sir Francis Drake? The convolutions of greed make no difference; still the mind reverts to the twenty-three hard-working seamen left to drown. They too must wait till the Day of Judgment to press their claim, perhaps immediately in the wake of the nobleman with his great scarlet cloak, and his wife in palest cream.

PART II

THE OTHERS

IX
An Atrocity

In stirring up so gigantic an accumulation as Admiralty Court proceedings—in whatever age, probably—one comes to realise, before much time has elapsed, the unpredictable, bizarre and often terrible nature of what comes tumbling out of pages gone dark yellow, long unopened and falling to bits along their edges. No matter that the writer's original intention has been to treat of piracy exclusively; such an intention, in the face of what one finds—of tragedy, farce, deceit, cruelty, even innocence and poetry—becomes less and less valid and, like the dry old paper itself, cracks and crumbles progressively.

One such case, in the tragic compartment, is that of Chimacha* (Chimache, Camatcha, Christian name not given) a Spanish merchant in a large way of business, presumably— presumption being based on the fact that he made shipping arrangements as much as a year in advance, something rarely encountered at the time. If evidence also includes hints and half-hints about shifty practices in which Chimacha had a hand, this might be true of many businessmen in all ages. Again the testimony in this case, like the *St Mary* multiple murder, reveals itself little by little; the period of the events cited makes it uncertain whether witnesses were lying, or had genuinely forgotten.

The first witness, one Carnabie, only speaks by hearsay, which always throws some haze of uncertainty on the proceedings. All the following took place at the port of Arenica, in Spain. Chimacha, he testifies, had entered into an agreement with one Johnson, owner of the *St John*, and Captain Moore, for a passage to England for himself, his wife, and a shipment of tobacco 'of 4000 l waight'. But through some hugger-mugger which Carnabie does not know or pretends not to know, a rival shipper and owner of another ship, one Captain Bruen, 'soe

* HCA 13–42—p. 7

prevayled with Chimacha that he shipped him self and his goodes
out of the *St John* and into the said other shipp.'

The sequel to the above is sudden, and perfectly astonishing.
By now the *St John* had arrived in Spain, fulfilling her engagement of a year ago with the merchant, only to find themselves
cheated of their contract. That the owner and possibly the
captain were outraged is understandable; what is really
mystifying is the manner in which the crew went out of control.
Whether Johnson and Moore tried to pacify them is never
mentioned; at any rate the men of the *St John* attacked the
rival ship *en masse* and 'did carie Chimacha on shoare out of the
shippe, and after he was executed, and his wife banished' set
at large?). At this point Carnabie hastily adds 'that he hath
hearde this', but has nothing more to contribute.

The next witness is John Bruen,* captain of the ship that
stole Chimacha's business from Moore. 'He knoweth that
Chimacha, a subiect of the King of Spaine, did in the river of
Menoca shippe about 4000 l wt of tobaccoe and wearinge
apparrel, and other necessaries for him selfe and his wife, to be
caried in the said shipp for England.'

Now he discloses an item that throws an additional murk over
the affair, though from first to last his statement is unsupported
by anyone else's. Remember again that Bruen—like Carnabie—
is speaking at a distance of time.

'This ex^ate knoweth of his owne knowledge,' he pursues,
*'that the tobaccoe and other goodes did not properlie belong to the sd
Chimatcha.* And he further saith that the sd Chimatcha was
afterwards by force fetched on shoare out of the sd shipp and
hanged, to this ex^ates knowledge, who sawe one hanged on
shoare, wch was said to be the sd Chimacha. He [Bruen]
knowing that the sd tobaccoe and other goodes were still in the
same shippe.'

Bruen's allegation that Chimacha had come into possession
of the tobacco through one crookedness or another, is unsupported throughout the testimony following. And if some
sort of cheating or worse were involved, who can say that he
deserved his fate?

One John Skelton who now takes up the tale is apparently—
by his final allusion—purser of Moore's ship. 'The sd shipp,'

* HCA 13–42—p. 32

he deposes, 'did staie in the river of Menoca a fortnighte after
the death of the sd Chimatcha, but none of the companie went
on shoare.' Understandably not; their position, after the
hanging, was somewhat delicate. Here one is prompted to ask,
where in this outrage was the Spanish law? Where were those
officers who showed themselves so furious and implacable
where port dues were concerned? But apparently no one lifted
a finger for the merchant and his wife. What does turn up is no
avenger, but a partner of Chimacha's; outside of this single
appearance he is never heard of again. 'Some Conference [took
place] with the merchante touching the Composition of the
shipment. And he [Skelton] tooke a servey of what goodes was
in her, and tooke a list of them as was rendered.'

The witness following, John fflaute, citizen of London,
throws a flood of light on the affair. He is now practising the
trade or profession of a barber-surgeon, which was his occupation on Moore's ship, and sounds like a man of probity—
sensible, and with an excellent memory.

'He affirms as true that in the yeare 1600 John Moore was in
trade of merchandise in the river of Menoca. In wch time and
place the sd Camatcha did agree with the sd Moore, that the sd
Moore should come the next yeare followinge with his shipp,
to fetch the sd Camatcha and his wife for England; and that he,
the sd Camatcha, would then lade into the sd Moore his shipp,
soe much tobaccoe as he could provide. And to this ex^ates
knowledge, whoe being chirurgeon of the shippe the *St John*,
was in her with the sd Captain Moore when the sd agreemente
was made. The sd Chimatcha him selfe,' he adds a clinching detail,
'did tell this ex^ate of the sd agreemente. He knoweth that the sd
Moore and companie did furnish and provide the *St John*, to
fetch the sd Chimatcha and his wife with tobaccoe, as covenanted.
But before the sd Moore his arrival at Menoca, Chimatcha had
shipped him selfe and his wife and a certaine quantitie of
tobaccoe into the other shippe of this ex^ates knowledge. He
heard that the sd Chimatcha was hanged and his wife' (banished?
blemished? this word appears twice but is hardly legible. The
assaulting crew could hardly have 'banished' the wife in her own
country. Could the word be a pseudonym for mass rape? With
men infuriated to the point of murder, anything is possible).

The witness fflaute, after the chief calamity, now delivers

himself of a statement less deadly, but odoriferous in its own right.

'He knoweth that the sd Bruen did not deliver [give back? return?] any goodes laden by the sd Chimatcha.' Probably not; he must have been hoping that with the owner dead, his possession of the tobacco would remain undisputed. Fat chance, with the crowd of cormorants involved. After some other questions have been put to fflaute on the value of the cargo, which he answers inconclusively—'more and lesse, accordinge to the goodnes of it'—he concludes his account by unveiling another fragment of the dirty story. 'He knoweth that certaine tobaccoe, in a chiste and in rolls, were brought out of the second shipp into Captain Moore's shipp, but,' prudently he withdraws from knowing too much, 'whether it was Chimatcha's tobaccoe or not, he cannot depose.'

What he means but will not say is, that Moore laid claim to part of Bruen's cargo as partial compensation for what he had been cheated of, and that Bruen—perforce—agreed. Such deals were so frequent that there is no keeping count of them. Commanders of rival ships, after the shouting and threatening stage of their rivalry was over, and to steer clear of further trouble, would almost invariably agree to a split of the disputed cargo; to a flat refusal, the only alternative was bloodshed.

Throughout all the testimony the attitude of the examining Judge, Sir Julius Caesar, is plainly to be divined—dissatisfied, and more and more outraged. Small wonder; old case or not, it *is* outrageous. The Examinations pile up and become mountainous, witnesses are subjected to repetition after repetition. Skelton for instance is hauled back to the stand two or three times, but has little more to contribute than an old but horrid detail. 'He saith that he sawe a thinge hange on shoare upon a paire of gallowes, wch was said to be the sd Chimacha', then adds, damagingly, 'that the sd tobaccoe was brought in the *St John* to England'—which would seem to mean that he had knowledge of the ship's trying to dodge the rigid port requirements of declaring cargo before unlading. Did he have it in for the owner or the captain, for some cause with which we are forever unacquainted? Something lurks in that needless statement on the 'sd tobaccoe'.

Again, in addition to the quality of this episode—the ugly

murder and ugly bargaining over cargo in sight of the body still swinging ashore—is one more item: the age of the case itself. The hanging and other events took place in 1600; the Admiralty procedure described took place in 1611.

But how account for a Court action eleven years after the event, or for any aspect of it? First of all, who were the plaintiffs? No mention of them ever appears, nor is this a simple case of owners versus pirates. And how did they scrape up witnesses, whom we might assume were long scattered? Not one of the seamen responsible for the murder ever appears. The presence of Carnabie, who only knows the affair at a remove, shows how hard up for testimony were the sponsors of the case. That they could get hold of first-hand testifiers like Bruen, Skelton and fflaute, is astonishing luck—but luck for which someone had to pay, heavily.

Nor can the verdicts and penalties (if any) be found; the Examinations themselves are incomplete. The fate of Señora Chimacha will always remain cloudy, unless it is she who is seeking (at such a remove?) damages of some kind. It seems that the exasperation of Justice Caesar will have to remain unsatisfied. Nothing is left but a lurking sense of apology for having made the ghost of Chimacha—crooked businessman or not—walk for one last time.

X

The Smooth Talker and the Dupe

This first sample of pure skulduggery is of a credulousness equally pure.* The case was heard before Sir Thomas Crompton on 4 August 1607; the first witness was 'James Motham, late M^r of the *Bonaventure*, examined [as to] what speche passed betwene him and a Jewe [never named from first to last] for the fraighting of the shipp at Cittamont in Argive.'

Richard Norgrave, merchant, must have had lading on the *Bonaventure*; the Jew also wanted to ship cargo with them. But Norgrave and Motham both, having had (presumably) some previous experience of him, 'and fearinge the sd Jewe would not pay, desyred securitie of him. Whereuppon the Jewe brought unto this d^pte a little box of wainscott, about half an ell longe and VIIJ inches depe, wherein the sd Jewe affirmed there was matter of importance and sufficient worth for the sd performance of the sd voyadge. And thereuppon the sd Jewe putt it into one of their emptye sackes wherein had beene corne, and sowed [sewed] it upp, and incked the same with inke over the sowinge, that it might be knowen yf it were opened.'

The Judge now put in a few questions: whether 'the box had Seales or no?' The witness 'sayeth it had not, but a lock.' Judge: 'Whether he sawe what was in it when it was delivered unto him by the Jewe?' Witness 'sayeth, he sawe it not opened.' Judge: 'What said the Jewe unto you, when he delivered it?'

It now develops that all this time Norgrave had been interpreting between Motham and the Jew, who had no English.

'Norgrave sayed,' witness continues, 'that the Jewe tould him he nedded not to knowe thereof, for there was a dedde man's head in it.'

This joking attempt to stave off the inquiry failed. Norgrave translated the answer to Motham, who—thick as he was—took

* HCA 13–97

no stock in it at all and reverted to the question of advance payment, saying 'that he demaunded of the Jewe, 100 £ or 200 £. And the Jewe [changing his tune] sayd that in the box delivered unto him, there was at the least soe much, or more.'

The Judge's next question discloses a picture, frenzied with jabbering and gesticulation, of a crooked dockside deal. 'Why did not the Jewe,' Sir Thomas asks, in effect, 'offer to take passage in your ship, along with his lading?'

The answer of Motham, though not too clear, reveals some dirty work—a shipboard scandal that had broken shortly prior to the *Bonaventure*'s arrival. When this other ship [unnamed] had anchored, some Jews aboard paid the merchant-owner in gold coin for their lading of corn; the merchant realized belatedly, when the corn was half unladed, that the coins were counterfeit. Not surprisingly he dropped the hatches on the rest of the corn, and one can imagine the pandemonium that followed. 'While the Jewes and the m'chaunt fell oute about the counterfett gould,' Motham pursues, 'the cheyff [wealthiest?] of the Jewes cominge aborde to fetch away the rest of the corne, hearing the quarell that was betwene the m'chaunt and the Jewes, putt of [off] in his boate and went away.' Very wise; he wanted nothing more to do with it. 'And manye of the [other] Jewes that were on borde, [hired] a boate and went with him. And the next daye,' Motham continues, reverting to the present, 'the m'chaunt Norgrave went a shore to ask the Jewe whether he would goe on the voyadge or noe, but he could not finde him.'

Again understandable, the modest withdrawal; the Jew had tried to talk his way into a free lading, and events may prove whether he had succeeded or not. As for his lack of an attempt to wangle for himself a free passage as well, it may be that he anticipated the nasty taste left in Gentile mouths from the counterfeit affair; no sense in pushing his luck too far.

By now Norgrave has given up his hunt for the Jew and returned to the ship, after which 'this d^pte hoysted saile,' Motham recounts, 'and came away, having the sd box in his custody still.'

Now appear several rifts within the lute, one of which was that things were not all that friendly between Motham and Norgrave.

'Being at sea,' the witness labours on, 'Norgrave demaunded the box. And this d^{pte} tould him that the Jewe had [taken] it away.' A barefaced lie, of course, followed up with a little bravado. 'And this d^{pte} [also] tould him that yf it *were* there the contents were his, and that he should have nothinge to doe therewith.'

He had removed the sack from its original hiding place (naturally), and tucked it away somewhere, though he had a long wait before he could get at it unobserved. From now on, with the painful revelations he was forced to make, he must have felt a considerable ass.

'Betwixte VIIJ and IX of the clocke in the eveninge,' he ploughs on, 'this d^{pte} cutt the Sacke and brake open the box in his cabon, none being bye.'

At this point he may have stopped dead; at any rate the Judge was obliged to prod him along with, 'What did you find in it?'

Actually there were two objects in the sack; the original account does not make this quite clear.

'Sayeth,' continues the tale, 'he founde a peece of brick wrapped upp in a clouthe. And uppon the openinge of the locke which was don uppon the halfe decke by his two mates, there was founde two little peeces of brick more, and nothing ells.'

Could the 'two mates' have been present during the first conversation with the Jew, and had Motham been obliged to cut them in on the contents of the box? Or—far more likely— had they been accomplices in something still strenuously unmentioned, so far?

'Being demaunded whether there was anye thinge ells in the box as guld [sic] Silver, perle or precious Stone in the sd box, he sayeth there was nothing more or other, than before.'

By this time we may suppose that the examining Judge was having a hard time to keep a straight face, and that the stenographer was able to hide his grins only by keeping his head bent over his writing. From here on, however, there is an entire lack of testimony in the affair—which does not inhibit reasonable suppositions: first of all, that Motham was lying throughout. Obviously he and Norgrave had connived with the Jew to give him free lading, and just as obviously this lading had been taken off, in England, without payment. But somehow the owner of the ship, getting wind of this transaction, had sued the merchant—Norgrave—as the best bet for damages. Or, on the other hand: if after the above sample of testimony the Judge had recommended that the case be thrown out of Court, we can hardly wonder. The signature to the examination, James Motham, is in good clear writing.

As for the person who—throughout the whole affair—had the last laugh, he has been visible once, but only in the beginning.

Zany Interlude

On a day of 1607, date illegible,* in some village a mile or two from London, one Thomas Brewster a sailor—and a low-grade one, if his future antics are any criterion—came into an ale-house and spread himself on to a bench; if the proprietress noticed what he put on the floor beside him she ignored it or pretended to, being well indoctrinated as to being too curious about her customers. Thomas began by asking the 'good wiffe' for a faggot, and she obliged. As he sat lighting his pipe, he asked her 'whether one Dier a porter did not dwele thereaboutes. And being tould that he dwelled at the next house, he desired her to call [him] to come and drinke with him. And so she came and called him' [whatever her sentiments about being used as a messenger girl] 'he being in his bedd.'

This first summons produced no effect; the time of morning is not mentioned, but a porter works hard and Dier—undoubtedly—needed his sleep. Brewster sat waiting, then apparently had the gall to ask the woman to try again; justifiably annoyed, 'she sente her daughter for him', but the daughter had no more luck than the mother. From this point we hear Dier's own account of what happened.

'At last the sd Brewster came to this d^{ptes} windowe and prayed him to come and drincke with him.' Dier was not proof against this specific invitation: 'And this d^{pte} arose and came, and they dranck two or thre potts togeather.'

After this they quitted the ale-house so that Brewster could 'gett his shoues [shoes] new soled'; Dier accompanied him, the two or three pots having put a lasting seal on their friendship. At this point Brewster evidently judged that Dier was

* HCA 13–97

sufficiently softened up for the delicate inquiry which had been his purpose from the first. 'He asked this dᵖᵗᵉ if he knewe eany frend that would buy a comodity wch he had, being waxe.' This was what he had put under the ale-house table, and had been carrying about ever since, no light burden. Wax 'in the cake'— like sugar in the loaf—weighed between thirty and fifty pounds. He must have had it wrapped in a tarpaulin or a bit of old blanket; wax is frequently mentioned in lists thieved from cargoes. Brewster went on to confide 'that he had stolen yt, and durst not make it knowen to every man.'

One might think not, knowing that his theft had put him within easy reach of the gallows. Yet the confession of theft failed to alarm Dier; either he was too stupid to appreciate the risk, or the memory of the two or three pots was still warm within him. So he answered the inquiry with 'He had no skill in such comodities, neyther knewe eany that had. Unlesse—' he was trying hard to be helpful, out of his dull brain '—unlesse John Lawe his land lord would buy it.'

Accordingly the delegation of two waited upon the landlord, 'having the cake of wax with them, and asked yf he wld buy the sd wax. And he said he had no use for it.' Mr Lawe possessed that much sense, anyhow. Yet, willing to do them a favour and seeing a friend of his, 'one Opes a chandler riding past the dore, he called him and asked yf he would buy the sd wax.' But Opes also had his wits about him; it could not be the first time he had been offered stolen goods. 'He looked on yt,' Dier continues, 'but would not buy yt, and so departed.'

After this, the local commercial possibilities having been exhausted, Brewster suddenly asked Dier 'to goe with him and carry the sd wax into London.' One might think that even Dier would have been warned by the two preceding refusals; but no, as invincibly unsuspecting and fat-headed as ever, he accepted both the heavy lump and the possibility of being caught with stolen goods upon him, 'and caried the wax as farre as Barkinge Churche.' The church must have indicated to Brewster some invisible boundary past which he was safe—or thought he was safe—for 'there he tooke the cake of wax againe, and sayd he would trouble him no further. And this dᵖᵗᵉ knoweth not where he disposed of the sd wax, or where he is at this present.'

Brewster's ship (or hoy most probably) was obviously

moored in the Thames well above Barking Church, and had as
obviously anchored there last night or very early that morning.
His trick of switching the burden from himself to Dier is a
piece of malignant low cunning; if they had been arrested while
Dier was carrying it, can there be any doubt that he would
have disclaimed all knowledge of it, and left Dier holding the
baby as well as the wax? This would probably have done him
little good—the captain of the hoy would have ultimately
identified him and the wax together—but the tactic is as
despicable as furtive. Also, Dier would have had a bad few
days in the Marshalsea, where the State—if it fed prisoners at
all—kept them at bare subsistence level. Yet again, the fact
that Dier was ferreted out as having associated with Brewster,
and grilled before the Admiralty Justice, means that the captain
of the hoy had lodged his complaint, and that the hunt was up.
Brewster's nasty cleverness indicates an experienced thief; one
would not mind if bad luck found him out, the sooner the better.

These, and thousands like them, are the people that Shakespeare saw and heard in his early ramblings about London. What
a pity, again, that the wax did not somehow find its way into
his writings.

SERVING A WARRANT

William Cottle* was a functionary or officer of the Admiralty;
his capacity is never precisely named. He is merely a faceless
being at the beginning of the following events, but it is interesting how during them his character reveals itself little by
little. The adventure itself, drab enough, illustrates the dangers
of carrying out a routine job when Englishmen were less
respectful and submissive to authority than now, and when this
lack of respect and submission could manifest itself in un-
pleasantly active ways.

Cottle, on a day in March 1614, had two warrants or summonses 'under the seale of the sd Courte, to arrest John Norris
of St Deacons in Somersett, and George Escott dwelling in
Mined' (Minehead). First he had to get out into the country;
a job pleasant or unpleasant, depending on the quality of his
horse and the state of the weather. Having arrived at St Deacons,

* HCA 13/97, p. 65

he called on Norris and tried to serve the summons. Its nature, aside from the demand for arrest, is never exactly stated, but by indications it seems clear that both Norris and Escott belonged to the comfortable middle class, country style. Norris, at sight of the warrant, instantly produced 'a special pardon under the greate seale of England', and told him to get out.

Cottle got out as ordered; by no means balked, only made wary by this first check to his efforts. He then went elsewhere and 'craved the advice of the portriffe' (portreeve: either a local mayor or a bailiff; he would have had first to find out the portreeve's name and his whereabouts). Having consulted him he then requested the portreeve to accompany him, and we can imagine how much the portreeve liked it—to be calling on neighbours or perhaps friends, in a threatening legal capacity. But he knew enough about his obligations to realise that he had no choice; the request of the officer of the Admiralty, bearing warrants, was not to be refused.

Accordingly the two men made their way to the house of the second addressee, Escott, and again Cottle attempted to serve the warrant. With remarkable promptitude Escott likewise whipped out 'a pardon under the greate seale of England, and an acquitance.' This action of Escott's suggests that both he and Norris were anticipating—for cause—some such descent upon them from the Admiralty, and had agreed on their tactics beforehand; the smell of collusion seems to hover on the air. But whether or no, the sight of this second pardon had no effect on Cottle. Standing his ground, he insisted on Escott's accompanying him 'to the house of one Lewis Lashbrooke, an attorney of the comon pleas in Mined.' It may have been the effect of the portreeve's presence that compelled Escott to go along as requested in the capacity of prisoner; also we can imagine in what frame of mind. 'And comming unto the house of the sd Lashbrooke,' Cottle's deposition continues, 'the sd Lashbrooke comanded this ex[ate] to gett him out of his doores, and sayd he had nothing to doe with the sd Escott.'

A shock for Cottle, the man of law taking sides (also by pre-arrangement?) with the prisoner. Nevertheless he refused to budge, saying 'that Escott was his prisoner, and he would not goe out of the house without his prisoner.'

At this point an unexpected combatant entered the fray. 'The sayd Lashbrooke's wiffe layd hands on this ex^ate, and would have thrust him oute of the doores,' Cottle continues, 'and used him very unkindly in wordes.'

How one regrets that a few of the words were not quoted, and while all this was going on Lashbrooke was advising the prisoner to consult 'a Justice of the peece or two, and gett a certificatt against him.' The four or five voices all speaking or shouting at once must have been invigorating music. In the face of this Cottle—presumably holding off the inflamed Mrs Lashbrooke with one hand, and retaining hold of Escott with the other—raised his voice over the uproar and 'chardged the portriffe with the sd Escott, and required both him and the sd Lashbrooke to looke to his prisoner.'

This was clever; he turned the tables on the reluctant portreeve and the abusive attorney by transferring to them the responsibility for the prisoner; back of him stood, unseen but not unfelt, the powerful presence of the Admiralty Court. 'Or else,' Cottle pursued in stentorian tones, 'they should answere for him.' Then he simply walked out on the lot of them, or in his own words, 'and soe departed.'

The sequel indicates a good deal of what followed. At least one hurried conference must have taken place between Lashbrooke and the two objects of the summonses, and we can imagine the tone of it falling from rage to reluctant reflection to reluctant submission; what use resisting an irresistible power? The affair ended with Norris and Escott entering 'into a bond of an hundreth pound to appeare in the Courte, when they should be called, uppon XX dayes warning.'

This whole episode, as warned of, is drab and petty, but it reveals the dangers of unpopular officials—the most unpopular being those unfortunates who had to gather in taxes of any sort; we remember the collectors of Ship Money (Charles I) who ran the gamut of severe manhandling by a mob, to injuries inflicted by flails and scythes. Cottle had nothing so formidable to face, but what he did encounter was unpleasant enough in its dimension of hatred and fury; his subdued persistence and subdued courage merit, at least, a subdued admiration. His signature, attached to his deposition, is in clear professional writing.

XI
Perils of the Sea

STORM

The three following accounts are of direst hardships of the sea, not in educated prose but in ordinary seaman's language. The first two narrators could not write, but made their mark; of the three who signed the third deposition (Disease) one at least retained—on the brink of infection and death—enough business sense to drive a pretty hard bargain when the danger was over, and who shall blame him? But it is the first account especially from which speaks that anguished voice—that distressing eloquence—extorted by deadly danger or even its memory, from the calmest, most inexpressive nature.

'Rogerus Clarck de Wappinge marriner'* (22 April 1600) of the *Rose Lyon*, informs us that his ship 'at Rochele did take on prunes and raisins, paper and other goods to be caried to London. And on the tuesday after, yt began to blow somewhat fryshe, and the next day yt grewe to a greate and tempestuous storme, insomuch that the shippe could not beare any saile from Wednesday midnight untill thursday morninge. And there came such abundance of water rakinge over the shippe and soe filled the Decke, that all the company stoode continually XXXV houres together at the pumpe, and bailinge oute water over the shipps sides.'

A wonder that those gigantic mid-ocean waves, battering and breaking over the small craft [180 tons at the biggest] did not sink at it once.

'And at the pumpe they labored with all their force for feare of their lives,' Roger continues, 'and did submitt themselves to death, for they made no account but that the shippe would founder under them. And if they had not labored continually during the storme, he verily thinketh they had all peryshed. Or yf it had not pleased god to mitigate the rage of the tempest in tyme, they had geven (given) over labour; for they were soe

* HCA 1–2—p. 188

overworne with the continuall labor that they could not have helde out much longer.'

Now, besides the storm, there loomed another terror.

'And besydes, they were nere the shore,' Roger tells, 'and feared greatly they should have byn driven into the shore and peryshed. And therefore the m^r took downe the foretop mast and rolled up the spritt yardes, thinking to make a riske to save them selves, for there were noe other remedy.'

Yet the *Rose Lyon* survived, Roger does not say how. He ends on a formula, still familiar. 'And he hath used [been accustomed to] the Seas about XII yeares space, and in that tyme hath byn in many stormes, but never was in the lyke for this tyme, nor never in more danger of peryshing.'

There seems no more evidence in the case of the *Rose Lyon*, though it comes to light that Roger 'was quarter master of the articulate shipp', and evidently a fine intelligent man. He makes his mark to the deposition: *RÇ*

ACCIDENT

The proportion of casualties great and small in the ships of the period was probably enormous; this is one aspect of maritime life that comes to the surface only intermittently, there being enough major disasters to engage everyone's attention. In 1800 St Vincent could say of a boatswain in Gibraltar dockyard, '[He has] masted 3 ships, using poor equipment, without hurting a man's finger', so even 200 years later a crop of unforeseen minor injuries was the normal and expected thing. The following incident, however, was by no means minor: the men giving testimony did their best, but it was—understandably—not enough.

The first witness bears the engaging name of 'Titus Crump, a marriner aged XXXIJ yeres'.* Titus relates 'howe Thomas Mourne, late M^r of the barck *Emily*, come by his death'. The barque, distressed by storms, cast anchor 'at the North foreland, and rid there fower or fyve howers. But the wind begun to rise, and the weather very foule and dangerous to bide there, and the

* HCA 1-2—p. 70

M^r caused the ankers to be wayed [weighed], to put into Ramsgate rode [road].

'And he took one handes pike,' Titus continues,' and this ex^ate an other, to wind about the windles (windlass), to bring the cable in and way the anker. And when they had wayed it about haulfe, the cable by reason of the foule weather heved upp, and the sd Mourne, standinge over his hande spike to way it done, put the windles about. And the shipp, with the foule weather, gave a gurck [jerk], and the hande spike beinge in the M^rs hande, with that gurck strieke [struck] the sd Mourne either under the gawes [jaws] or eare, that he lett go his handes, and with the roule of the shipp fell presently [instantly] over borde.'

The thunderbolt, paralysing, but not to these brave men.

'And this ex^ate,' Crump pursues, 'being on the other side of the windles and seeinge him fall, ran with all the hast he could to ketch hould of him, and [managed to] touch his back.'

With all Crump's effort, however, he had the sea, the storm and the ship against him.

'But before he could gett hould of him,' he proceeds, 'the barck with the rowling of the sea arose upp again, so that this ex^ate could not come nere him. And before the barck with the next wave came downe againe, the sd Mourne was driven under the bowes of the shipp.'

The description of the ship, flung up to the crest of the wave in one instant, and pitching into its gulf in the next, is enough to induce seasickness even in the land-dweller.

'And afterwardes,' he concludes, 'he could never sett eyes of [sic] him.'

The horrid account ended, Crump does his best, very attractively, to exonerate others of the crew who witnessed the accident.

'The others of the company were houlding the cable as this ex^ate and the M^r were winding yt yn. And if they should have lett their handes goe,* the cable might needs have run out again. And by that occasion they could not save the sd Mourne, he was soe suddenly heved over borde.'

Crump, again, does not write: he makes his mark, H.

---

* So expert a source as Commander Peter Kemp confirms that an anchor running out suddenly, in storm conditions, is very dangerous.

DISEASE

Sickness of every kind, aboard ship, was another chief nightmare of marine existence. Scurvy and typhus, as we know, were the chief visitants, the first from vile food and water gone slimy in the cask, the second from infestation of the typhus louse in clothes and bedding. The exact cause of the example here quoted however,* does not precisely chime with the two afflictions mentioned. The rate at which this unknown malady killed is a little too devastating for scurvy; it might have been typhus, but the results of it sound more like a massacre than an illness. In the Admiralty Court hearings no effort was made, apparently, to put a name to this devastation. To one person it has rather the sound of a galloping influenza, which mows down whole populations like fire in dry brush. It may be noted that, in the rescuers' testimony, no case of subsequent infection is ever mentioned among them; we can only suppose, at a distance of 400 years, that the deadly thing had run its course.

The first witness (14 August 1612) is 'Jacob hendrickson of horne in Holland, gonner, who saith by chardge of his oath that he was in the shipp the *Jacob* of Newhavon, in his late viadge; and there went 52 men in the said shipp. And they had byn gon 9 or 10 moneths, on the same viadge.'

Now, without further preamble, he plunges into disaster.

'At that tyme *the Captain, m*^{r}*, pilott, boateswaine, surgeon, Steward, pilotts mate, Carpenter and his mate, and all the officers of the shipp, were dead; and others of the mariners to the number of 36 persons.* [Writer's italics.] And 8 [others] were verie sicke, and only 8 able to stand on their leggs and handle the sails. And of them, this ex^{ate} and 2 ffrench men had a little knowledge to guide the helme, and no more.'

Now suddenly, 'by gods grate mercy, this ex^{ate} had syght of 3 shippes.' Instead of haling them madly however Jacob took council with his half-dead company, 'whether they should make towards them and seeke relefe, or no.'

Opinion was obviously divided; some were afraid 'for that if they were Spaniardes, they knewe they should all dye.' Apparently it was Jacob who took on himself the responsibility: 'of two evills, they might choose the leaste rather, to fall into their

* HCA 1–6–78

ennemies handes than perishe in the sea. And uppon that
resolution this ex^ate shott off a peece, and strucke his foretop
sail. And thereuppon'—marvellous moment '—the sd shipps
stayed for them, and releved them.'

The 'sd shipps' turned out to be English; the 'relefe' was so
prompt and generous that, again, it dispels any suspicion of
familiar infectious illness. Or if it had been plague, whose
external signs were known to everyone, they would have run
for their lives. As it was, ten of the sick company were carried
into one of the English ships, ten of the English were put in
charge of the *Jacob*, 'and therein they were broughte into the
city of London.'

This was really noble, by the tough standards of the sea. Nor
is it an unreasonable guess that no one but the English would
have acted so; Spaniards or pirates would have thrown sixteen
enfeebled men overboard and taken possession of the *Jacob*.
Still, some bargaining had taken place during the voyage to
London, nor is there any hint that Jacob—or others of his crew
who testified—found this at all objectionable.

'In consideration of that favor, chardges, and their mens
wages,' Jacob acknowledges freely, 'this ex^ate and the rest of the
company livinge were contented to give the m^r one hundreth
and fifty pounds.' He does not say 'or give them the equivalent
in value', but the subsequent proceedings make the terms of the
agreement clear. At once 'we delivered them such goodes as are
set downe in the first skedle hereunto annexed,' says Jacob; it
was all very businesslike. 'And we promised to deliver them
such other thinges belonging to the said shipp, as should make
upp the said some [sum].' He then goes on to affirm 'that this
contracte was made upp on the high seas and agreed uppon
with the expresse consente of his company then livinge, *and at
their ernest entreaty*.' And why not? They owed their lives to the
English ships, and they knew it. He expresses the direct doubt
that any of them would have survived if the English ships 'had
not mett with the *Jacob*, and releved her.' The statement is
signed not only by Hendrickson, but by one Green and one
illegible.

As to the occasion which prompted this testimony, and which
is never mentioned again in the following evidence, again we
are privileged to guess a little. To the owners of the *Jacob*,

£150 was an excessive price to pay for sixteen men's lives; they must have sued to recover it. Part of the answer to them lies in Hendrickson's testimony, and part in the depositions of two other young survivors. The first one, Peter Brunsway?* gives his age as being 'twenty-three or thereaboute' (very common) and describes himself as being 'of deepe marine' (very uncommon). The second man, Peter Corbeline,† is twenty-four; 'only a saylor and no officer' in the *Jacob*. The testimony of both may be combined: 'the survivors of the company were in miserable and desperate cast, the Captaine and all their officers deade, and of the 16 left most of them were sicke, and had no knowledge to guide the shipp. And if they had not met with the English shipps they had peryshed in the sea, or byn cast among the Spaniardes their ennemies.' Both lads agree that 'the English shipps, finding what wofull distresse they were in, did spare 8 or 10 of their company to bring the sd *Jacob* into some porte of England.' Also they have both seen the contract, 'firmed [confirmed] by Peter Brunsway his marke, and by the rest of the company, and was freely and willinglye agreed uppon, and the contents thereof are most true.'

It is the second Peter, Corbeline, who adds a serious footnote as to the risks the English ships had taken: indirectly of disease, also in lengthening their voyage by the life-saving interlude. 'The *Jacob* was aboute two degrees from the equinoctial lyne' (sounds hot) 'and the English shipps were kepte at sea the longer, by reason of the *Jacob*.' This delay might have brought on scurvy or other sickness incidental to too-long voyages at sea; Corbeline is the only one who mentions this, intelligent boy. Both young men testify through an interpreter. The date of the hearing is a Sunday; again a day of no rest for Justice Mr Doctor Trevor, who conducts the examination. Knowing the strenuous fairness of the Court of Admiralty, it is hardly conceivable—when the case came to trial—that the English seamen should not keep firm hold of their hundred and fifty pounds.

By the way, there exists the note of a ship‡ which was genuinely plague-stricken (plagam mortalem profunditatis); unfortunately this is torn and half-effaced. It concerns the trial of a 'Sayler, Robert Jones', and at the bottom of the Inquiratur:

* HCA 13–42—p. 75   † HCA 13–42—p. 76   ‡ HCA 1–5—no. 30

'He was sentenced by the Court to be hanged, but yet was reprieved [reprovatus] and held back from death.'

Nothing more, except that Robert owned a knife, value fourpence—for whatever light that may cast on the scene.

XII
Two-Faced John Exton

To patch together the exploits of men like John Exton from the broken record of Examinations, Inquiratores, Warrants and so forth, is not a satisfying method of biography. Yet this scoundrel has, in a sense, left such conspicuous tracks through the Admiralty records—footprints that join others, separate, fade, go into hiding and reappear over a number of years— that one begins to pursue them, first out of curiosity, secondly out of a growing and ardent hope that the gallows will catch up.

Of the men who were associated in the random pirate sense— sometimes joined in pillage, violence and murder, sometimes acting independently—Exton seems the most dangerous, resourceful and cunning. He was one of those men who lead a double life; in his case successfully, for many years. He was at one and the same time actively a pirate, also a respectable married man who had an ownership in the legitimate business of cargo ships, both for import and export. The combination may have been frequent beyond knowledge; Raleigh and Drake were famous examples of the pattern, both having interests in legitimate and pirate ships. There are indications that Exton's wife—a worthy partner—knew all about both his professions; she enters the scene later on, briefly but tellingly. The allusions to Exton, especially in the Admiralty Court Acts, are numerous beyond description, since the crimes of which he was guilty involved, likewise, a countless number of lesser criminals who acted under his command; one feels in him a remarkable power of authority and fearlessness. As a merchant he was called Mr Exton; in his piratic capacity, Captain Exton.

An early distinct trace of John and his doings is dated 1607,* when his ship (unnamed) attacked the *Hopewell* 'of kinsala in Ireland'. Not only were the *Hopewell* and her passengers plundered, but a member of the pirate crew, John Bannister, is indicted 'for assistinge one William Sante in the killinge of a

* HCA 1–5—143B, no. 12

man unknowen, on borde the sd *Hopewell'*. Exton, in this particular adventure, remains modestly in the background, only being mentioned for stealing 500 chests of sugar from another victim, the *Mermaid*. One may assume that the court, as yet, has no inkling of his real quality, but the awakening is not long delayed. In a following document, an Inquiratur marked True Bill, are the names of the pirate ships in which he operated: 'John Exton of the parishe of St James near Taunton in the County of Somersett, in the *Tomasin* and the *Talbott*, did upon the *Serena* comit piracies and felonies and maltreat and menace those in her.' The next document, also an Inquiratur, conveys in accents of brass the charge of murdering our old friend ffaveras, 'of malice aforethought' (progitata). The murder was during the reign of Elizabeth I and these Inquiratores are dated 1607 and 1608; it took that long to catch up with him.

The trial of Exton rocks us back on our heels. With all the weight of piratic evidence against him (some of it 'confessed by him selfe'); even with the murder allegation; the document is marked *Ignoramus*. Our disappointment might be more alleviated if the document itself were not so badly defaced, the right hand edge being blackened and totally illegible. Enough of it survives, however, to assure us that John got a stiff prison sentence: 'the sd John Exton, after deliberation . . . in the sd gaol of the Marshalsea [Carcarus Mariscaltiae]' can be made out.

Promptly on the news of the incarceration, however, come two other documents,* both breathing outrage. The first makes clear that John has escaped, the second that he has (as usual) involved someone else in his trouble: 'in breakinge gaol he hath persuaded and procured one William Richardson to obtain rope and hookes, that he might escape.' How the attempt failed is not indicated, but all too evidently John is back in the Marshalsea. Next is a long list ominously headed 'piratts to be arraigned in Southwarck the 7th of June 1607', with Exton's name on it, and after that another tale of offenders† exhibits the name of Richardson as 'accessory for the escape of John Exton oute of the Marshalsea, confessed in pte by him selfe', and also displays the names of two witnesses against him. Was he a gaoler? If so, did this betrayal of the State involve the gallows? Nothing tells us one way or the other, but of one thing we can be sure: Exton

* HCA 1–5–150–1   † HCA 1–5–187

could afford to bribe, handsomely, a poorly paid lower official whose daily surroundings were rags, starvation, filth, smells and despair. Small blame to him if he were unable to resist a substantial money inducement from so accomplished and so persuasive a rascal.

The next indication of John's restless career (at one remove) is the hauling up of his wife, Thomasin, before the Admiralty Judge; we remember that one of his ships was called *Thomasin*. This new document,* not dated, makes it impossible to tell whether it pertains to his first escape, or a later one; over all the years when the Examinations or Acts give a quick glimpse of him, he was in trouble with the law. The only thing that comes across clearly, in this grilling of Mrs Exton, is the woman herself. A cool customer, also a tough one; unflurried, obviously not impressed by the Judge, and—in the face of his harsh insistent questioning—imperturbably offering her claims of total ignorance, while hinting, in the most oblique way possible, that she knows more than she is telling and might tell it if any advantage to her husband were guaranteed. An abbreviated version of this duel between the Judge and the wife follows, with the wife winning on all counts.

'Being demaunded whether she lay with her husband the nighte he went a way [escaped], she saith she did not, but he coming into the chamber unto her, willed her to goe to bedd and to pull the bolt. Wch she did accordingly; since wch tyme she saw him not. And she doth thincke it was about two of the clocke in the morninge when she herde them crye out of his escape.

'Being asked where her sd husband lay that nighte after he escaped oute of prison, sayeth she knoweth not where he lay.

'Being asked what day she bought and brought the Ropes to make a scaling ladder for her husband, Sayeth she brought them unto him uppon Saturday last in the after noone. But whoe made them into a Ladder she knoweth not, for she was abroad uppon Sunday all day. And where she bought them or of whom, she knoweth not [likely].

'Being asked what became of certain papers that her husband had arranged the accompte betweene her and her husband and Marninge: [Marninge was alternately John's accomplice and

* HCA 1–5—p. 22

business partner] Sayeth, she knoweth not. But sayeth, *yf these can be made meanes for her husbands libertye, she doth not doubte but she will bring them forth.*'

This, to one hearer at least, sounds like the most staggering insolence. Yet the Judge, instead of committing her for contempt, tries one last time to trap her.

'Being demaunded where her husband appoynted her to mete him':

One can see Thomasin's inward smile at this feeble effort, as she responds smoothly: 'He appoynted her noe place.'

Now begins a rapid merry-go-round of inquisitions on various associates of Exton. Evidently the Court would like to pass the capital sentence on him, but as evidently they have (in some way or other) insufficient material. Therefore they pounce on a first examinee, 'Richard Staddinge* of Fairwaye in Devon'. Of him one can honestly say he is assiduous as a prison visitor—as to frequency and peculiar hours, both.

'Being demaunded how manye tymes he hath been with the sd Exton in pryson, saith: he hath beene with him every other daye. And yesterday beinge Sunday, sayeth he was twyse with him, about VJ oclock in the morning and VIJ in the evening.'

'Being demaunded whether he knoweth one John Haye nowe prysoner in the Marshalsea, sayeth he hath spoken with him dyvers times *in the companye of the sd Exton*, but other familiar-itye he hath not with him.'

The Justice tries again: does he know 'Mr Maninge, prysoner at Mr Popes in St Catheryn (a sponging house?) Sayeth, he wente thyther to borrow 21 sh of Mr Maninge for the sd Exton, whych he refused to lend him.' Very sensible of Manning, but why would the well-to-do Exton need a guinea?

At this point the Judge gives up on Staddinge and switches to one Josias Scaddon. Josias has also been visiting Exton in prison, but with good reason. 'He was last nyght with him about ten of the clocke at nyghte.' Flexible visiting hours indeed, but he had to give Exton bad news about the recovering of his liberty. Josias denies totally any connection with Exton's escape, and signs his deposition in a small literate hand.

With Abraham Collins however—a few days later—a

* HCA 13/97

considerable quantity of dirt comes home to roost.* Collins is a Dutchman residing at Middleburgh; his evidence is antagonistic and bitter. 'He doth well know Exton, whoe was Captaine of the *Greene Dragon*,' he begins. 'And beinge sente for by the sd Exton, he came on borde the sd shipp, and was forcibly kepte and caried to Sea against his will. And they tooke from subiects of the King of Spaine four hundreth and forty chestes of sugers, and fyve and twenty tonnes of Brasile woode, against this dptes will.'

He proceeds to spill other information which he has gathered in the course of the voyage. 'In fflushinge, Exton hath one Balthasar Stephens, who [passes] for Captaine of the *Greene Dragon*.' This quick change may be useful, presumably, in case of an arrest or accusation. 'Howbeit,' Collins sweeps away this claim, 'the sd Exton was Captaine at Sea, and no other comaunded during the viadge.' He then gives further proof that he has not wasted his time aboard ship; he identifies by name a large part of the crew of sixty, and testifies that 'they were in the sd shipp the *Dragon*, at the taking of the sd sugers.'

Having contributed these hopeful nails to Exton's coffin he makes way for another witness, Richard Stafford (unidentified) who also has plenty against Exton. He confirms the piracy of sugar and wood, and offers the valuable information that the owners of the *Green Dragon* were 'Mr Maninge and Captaine Exton, victuallers and setters furth of the sd shipp.' He also produces bits of biography and worse: 'He knoweth that Exton was ymprisoned at fflushinge by a man of Amsterdam for moneys taken from him at Sea; who bayled him so he was dischardged, he knoweth not.' But he *does* know where Exton got the money to repay the Amsterdamer: *'he payd it out of the companyes share of the prize.'*

The crew, naturally, was not taking this lying down. Exton had disappeared, again naturally, so a number of them called on Manning to protest, and got nowhere. 'They fell oute with him that they could not have their moneys, and called him cosoner [cozener—cheat]. And said they would make him knowen to be the shipps owner.' Much good this threat did them where Manning was concerned. 'He sware a greate oath that he *was* owner, and cared not yf all the world knew of it.' Now Stafford,

* HCA 13—pp. 42, 45, 51

in the onrush of revelation, offers a bit of scandal: 'The sd
Maninge was acquainted with such a [some] woman, and had a
child by her.' Having got this off his chest he is obviously
exhausted. 'He cannot declare more.'

All this had been going on since 15 August 1607. By 1
September Exton, who is again in the Marshalsea's loving
arms, has visitors: William Bullion, Mr Guerin, and Mr Beau.
Bullion is merely a friend who—incidentally—happens to have
excellent hearing; of the other two, one at least is no envoy of
loving kindness. 'Wee were levinge the prison,' Bullion
testifies. 'And I did heare Mr Beau offer Mr Guerin, for a
composition [arrangement, compromise] for the sd John Exton,
the sum of XL¹ in hande and XX¹ at a certaine daye. Wich the
sd Guerin refused.'

Naturally he refused; 'the sd Guerin' had told Bullion (at
what date is not revealed) that Exton had made a foolish and
uncharacteristic mistake—of admitting 'that he was at Sea when
they did robb the sd Guerin of his ship and goodes.' Such a
confession would hardly serve as prelude to an amicable
settlement. Moreover, Guerin values his losses at £200; the
offer of £60 in full repayment has so infuriated him that he
pours out the whole story of the attempted 'composition',
incidentally bringing a new name into the picture—one Jarmin,
obviously a tool or subordinate of Exton's. Here Thomasin
Exton makes her entrance likewise—not in person, but only by
way of her agent. 'The sd Jarmin, meeting Mr Guerin in
Cheapside, did tell him he was required by the wieffe of the sd
Exton, to see if he could compounde with him for £40.' This
was not even a down payment, but was to be due 'at Michmas
[Michaelmas] nexte.' Small wonder if Guerin laughed in his
face while refusing, 'sayinge he would not take a penny lesse
than two hundred poundes'.

The abortive attempt, all the same, reveals Thomasin's
alertness, her watchfulness, and—more to the point—her up-
to-date knowledge of Exton's affairs. He must have been in
secret communication with her all through the period of his
imprisonment, his escapes and his other disappearances;
keeping her informed of day-to-day claims and claimants, and
giving her instructions how to deal with them. However black
was Exton's career, he had a devoted wife—unless behind it of

course was mere self-interest, but one would prefer the first alternative.

From here on (1607) we have a dizzying accumulation of writs up to 1613; they are still trying to get him on the same charges, piracy and murder. All at once (19 April 1613): 'petition for pardon for John Exton.' We know that this was refused; not through any surviving document, but by the number of writs against him that continued piling up through 1618 to 1620, and after that to 1627. On none of these writs—twenty-eight of them have been examined—is any penalty noted, but at least they never stopped trying.

As for the record of his end, there is no record—which does not prevent falling back on our old resource, conjecture. Exton, by all indications, was a fairly prosperous man when the governmental hunt for him really hotted up in 1607 after the gaol-break; his next twenty-three years, to say nothing of his money, were spent in dodging the law by every stratagem at his command. Such manoeuvres are expensive; can a man forced to dissipate his resources in this fashion ever again replace what he has spent? Can he ever again have time to devote to his business legal or illegal, with the hot breath of pursuit always on his neck? By 1627, also, he must have been an old man of fifty or so, as old age was reckoned at the time. If the nervous strain of his situation had not worn him out by then, the attrition of his means must have guaranteed him a comfortless death.

For us, not for Exton, might be suggested one questionable compensation: if there is no record of his actual end one might assume that he caused—among the Justices and other officials of the Admiralty Court—a high rate of mortality from sheer exhaustion.

XIII
A Bungler

If Exton is a clever or even a brilliant villain, John Poindexter 'of Brillet',* surely qualifies as either half-witted or totally witless, take your pick. It is easy to believe that, in his life prior to this episode, he had been a thief, but a casual or careless thief; it took this simple but dazzling exploit to hoist him into the knowledge of the Admiralty Court and to an easy view of Wapping's speciality.

On a day of 1610 John, loitering in a seaside area not named, fell in with a boatload of six men; they might have been casual acquaintances, and equally they might have been totally unknown to him. Casually he wished himself aboard their boat, and as casually accepted an invitation to visit the *Golden Calf*, a small ship of 30 or 40 tons moored nearby. The seven of them went aboard according to plan; the shipper and his trumpeter were there, 'as well as fyve dutch men who were also aborde.' The shipper must have had some acquaintance with this impromptu foray, since he greeted them without suspicion and brought out the bottles. 'We fell in drinkinge,' Poindexter testifies, 'and in aboute an howers space we putt the shipper and his trumpeter ashore, as well as the fyve dutch men, and sett saile toward St Ellyns pointe.' The eviction scene must have been more or less lively, depending on whether the Dutchmen were sober enough to join resistances with the shipper and trumpeter. Whether or no the intruders won, and—obviously skilled enough to handle small craft, like most shore dwellers—they steered toward the Point and anchored. By next day they had recruited, ashore, some kindred spirits, how many not mentioned. After this they sailed for the Isle of Wight, to find others who might be interested in joining; this effort got them two more. Having obtained a ship by the simplest and most direct means, with equal simplicity and directness they were now collecting a pirate band.

There now appeared (presumably) a problem: the ship was

* HCA 1–6—p. 171

in cargo at least partially, to judge by what followed, but was not victualled, and for this money must be obtained. By this time, in this gang of louts and scruffs, there had been some informal division into officers and crew. Among these officers 'there was some secrett talk', Poindexter continues, with the result that two of them went ashore again; we are not informed, at this point, whether they were still anchored off the Isle of Wight or off Portsmouth, but most probably it was the latter. In any case the two shore visitors came back in the evening 'with XXX[1] in Spanish money and gould.' Stolen undoubtedly, and besides they had got their hands on 'aboute fiftye peeces of duch grogrammes [grosgrains], bayes, sayes [silks] and buskins', for which a customer appeared at once, some merchant or receiver: 'he boughte the moste of it and caried it awaye in a boate.'

By now Poindexter's feeble wits were stirring, but on a point—characteristically—of minor importance. Still, he was sufficiently disturbed over it to go to the (so-called) captain, one William Rawlyns, and to demand 'howe the sd goodes could be taken ashore and not discovered?' (i.e., by the Customs). Rawlyns, with the most admirable sangfroid, explained that the buyer 'had a key of the Round Tower without the gate, and there might laye' whatever goods he pleased. This clear evidence of corrupted customs officers restored Poindexter to a sweet calm, and he made no further comment when the same buyer 'came on bord at other tymes and caried away goodes in sackes, how much he knoweth not.'

By now the glorious news of this treasure trove had got all around Portsmouth, with the result that the ship was inundated with buyers, some of them respectable officers. 'The Town Clerck of Portsmouth came on borde and bestowed fyfteene pounds for the sd goodes, which this ex^ate saw paid to Rawlyns on the Decke. Also Richard Stockwell the goner [gunner] of Portsmouth, and his mate, came on borde.'

By now, likewise, the purchasing public had taken the measure of the ship's crew—their fecklessness and abysmal ignorance of values—and from now on most transactions fell abruptly from purchase to barter. One merchant, though 'he bestowed a little money on the sd Rawlyns, had comodities for 2 barrells of beere, a muskett and a pistoll.' It seems that word had got around that beer was a powerful argument, for among other buyers from Radcliffe and Stokes Bay appears one John Tokens 'who brought with him 2 barrells of beere and six musketts' (probably unusable). This large-hearted soul was so pleased with his bargain that he promised 'to bring a man on borde, who should bestowe one hundreth pounds on the sd comodities.'

Poindexter now estimates the length of his stay in the ship as 'aboute ten days after the taking thereof; and the other six continued on borde the lyke tyme, to his knowledge.' He willingly gives the names of three of these, but 'the names of the other three he knoweth not', and adds that the ship had in her 'XXIJ or XXIIJ packes of the sd comodities and a Trunck with pictures [a painted chest?], and nothing ells to his knowledge.' He signs himself, engagingly, as *John poindexter alias*; better writing than one would expect from such a fool.

So much for his statement; now comes the Interrogatory by the Judge himself. As often happens, circumstances begin to appear that Poindexter has modestly suppressed, one of them relating to at least one pirate cruise made in the stolen ship during her career of ten days. Now in some manner he is forced to admit 'that beinge at Sea in the *Goulden Calfe*, they haled a ffrench man, and the ffrench man made a shott and killed one of the men in the *Calfe*.'

This sounds like a lie; attacked merchant ships seldom fired till they were fired upon.

'Whereuppon,' the witness continues, 'this exate and company shott againe two shotts with one of the murtherers.'

Guns like this seem unusually heavy equipment for a little ship of 30 or 40 tons.

'And one of the ffrench men was killed,' the dire story continues, 'having the fore pte of his hande shott away with a murthering peece. And died presently [at once], and laye on the hatches aboute fower houres after he was deade, before he was throwen over borde. With a waight made fast to him as is usuall at Sea, lest,' he explains affably, 'otherwise he should flote.'

He signs himself, this time, as JP alias bellet [sic]. Does his fate seem in any doubt? Too bad it caught up with him after the *Golden Calf*, and not before.

XIV
The Charge of Cowardice

Testimony in this case,* incomplete, begins with Spanish ships making an assault on two English merchant ships, the *Cherubim* and the *Angel*. If the Spaniards were not pirates, their intent was surely partly piratic. An English ship, the *Ascension*, went to the rescue. In some manner of which there is no record, and which we cannot fathom, one Kirkman of the *Ascension* was charged with running from the enemy. The person or persons who made it are never named in writing or by the witnesses, but to make up for this lack we have the grandest chorus possible of shipmates who spoke in his defence. This is very reminiscent of the charge of 'avoiding combat' brought, almost 200 years later (1779) by Admiral Palliser against Admiral Keppel, except that the later trial involved officers of the highest rank. But the spirit of the testimony in both cases is its unanimity of defence, its tremendous whole-heartedness. What Kirkman's precise standing was is also never mentioned, but he must have been either the master or the chief gunner; his ship, and the two ships he was protecting, were presumably too small to warrant captains. In this combat were five Spanish ships against three English.

'George Wood of Ratcliffe, mariner and late m^r of the *Angell* of London, sworne and examined, sayeth: There were very many shotts made out of the *Ascention* at the fyve Spanish shipps nere Gibraltar in may last, for the fyght continued betwixte them aboute fyve howers space. And during the fyght there was no sparing of powder, of his certaine knowledge. And the m^r and company of the *Ascention* fought and turned againe and fought, and showed themselves like men, and did not run away or worck like cowardes. And this d^{pte} *knoweth* that at the beginning of the fyght the *Assention* [sic] was the hend [hind] most shipp and might have gon away, if the M^r had so intended. But did not, but cast about and came amongste the other

* HCA 13–34—p. 271

English shipps, and did their endevors and helped to reskue them; and gott to wind warde of them all, nexte [nearest] to the Spaniardes, and fought with them as aforesaid.'

Now John Spencer, master's mate of the *Angel*, backs him up.

'As soon as Mr Kirkman sawe the Spanishe shipps following after in the enterrance out of the Straintes and set uppon the *Cherybin* and the *Angell*, he tooke in his top sailes and cast aboute and foughte, and shewed them selves not as cowardes; for yf they had byn such men, they might have gon their wayes at their pleasure, and never have byn in any danger of the Spaniardes.'

Thomas Bushipp, trumpeter of the *Angel*, more or less repeats the above, but adds a detail of the fight's termination: 'As soone as one of the Spaniardes had received a broad side and had fallen off, two others of them tacked aboute to get the wether gage of the English shipps; but belike not finding them selves fitted, came no more upp with them. And so,' he concludes, 'Mr Kirkman bare away through the Straites mouth, and the other English shipps with him, and went their wayes.'

From Henry Challicombe, next witness, we have a nice contemporary phrase: 'Mr Kirkman *never offered to run lucky* [get away safe], but plied uppon them with ordinance, in the best manner.' Henry sounds like a connoisseur. 'And he thinketh,' he pursues, 'it had byn wronge [gone badly] with the *Cherybin*, if the *Assention* had not come.' He signs with a trembly HC, evidently not caring to essay the perils of Challicombe. Then George Gibson, ship's surgeon, affirms the same and makes a grand conclusion: 'He *sawe* the forwardnesse of Mr Kirkman, in that same fyght.'

It remains for John Paule of Ipswich to give some interesting statistics: 'One hundreth and fifty great shell were dischardged out of the *Assention*, and at the least forbye, the number of Cartarges [cartridges] given out, were not lesse. And Mr Kirkman,' he states nobly, 'showed him selfe as a faithfull frende to his Cuntry men,' then passes to the last melancholy item, which one would expect to have come from the surgeon: 'There were thre men slaine in the *Assention*, of his knowledge.'

Like the court-martial of 200 years later, it seems that this unanimous repudiation of the cowardice accusation—undoubtedly inspired, like the Keppel-Palliser affair, by jealousy and hatred—must have resulted in the complete exoneration of Kirkman. One can only hope that the accuser, in his turn, got into trouble.

A Local Clash

This particular encounter rested firstly on a point of marine etiquette, and secondly on the flourishing hatred between the English and the Scots. This had by no means faded up to the beginning of the nineteenth century, and at our present period of time—22 April 1600—was in fullest and most refulgent bloom. Thirdly, what began as a patriotic demonstration ended in piracy, or call it at least semi-piracy.*

The incident had taken place in January, five months earlier, when—by testimony of Johes Johnson of Odenwayse—'the *Reprisal* mett with a scottishe shipp cominge from Palma, and Captain Croker of the *Reprisal* haled the sd shipp and comanded the company there of to jenke [lower sails] for the Queene of England. Which the company of the scottishe shipp denied, and with a naked sword deseired the *Reprisal* to beeware. Whereuppon they fell to fyght, and the sd scottishe shipp was in the ende taken by the *Reprisal*. And therein were diverse scottishe men, an English man and a duch boye, and confessed that in Palma they were laden with goodes, and nowe were going to Grenwiche for the rest of their ladinge.'

It is the 'duch boye' who informs Johnson that 'the sd shipp did belong to one Ager Dento a Spaniarde who was on borde'. Chattily he adds 'that forty pipes of wine and thirtene chestes of suger were taken out of the scottishe shipp into the *Reprisale*', before coming up with two unexpected items. 'He sayeth that Captain Croker, at the requeste of the scottes, waifted them to the Roade of Teneriff, for fear of other men of warre. And that Captain Croker gave them a maine drabler† and a forebonnet which they stude in need of.'

Why these sudden gestures of amity? For the same reason previously encountered; Croker was beginning to suspect that he had gone too far, and with good reason. The next witness, Octavio Deneto, is now examined through an interpreter, and

---

* HCA 13–34—p. 176
† A piece of canvas laced to the bottom of a sail called the bonnet.

begins bringing to light incidents that have been glossed over.

[Deneto] 'knoweth the *Reprisale* in January last mett with a shipp and haled her, demaunding of whence she came, and some answered they were of Scotland, and Captain Croker comanded them a maine for the Queene of England. And one standing in the poope showed a naked sworde sayinge, a maine, noe, you villaines. And a shott came first from the scottishe shipp which killed the m^{rs} mate in the *Reprisale*, and hurte the Captain in the hande and an other in the hande also. And the *Reprisale* answered with shott againe, and after some fyght took the sd scottishe shipp.'

Deneto* now describes some transactions which—apart from the gift of the drabler and bonnet and a convoy of sorts to Tenerife—testify to Croker's increasing nervousness over the affair, his awareness that Elizabeth's laws concerning attacks on friendly powers were not merely decorative, and the stratagems which he devises to protect himself as much as possible. The witness confirms that Croker certainly took wine and sugar from the Scottish ship, but softens it with:

'The scottishe Captain and his leftenant came on board the *Reprisale*.' [An enforced visit?]'And they confessed voluntarily that nothinge was taken from them appertayning to the sayling of the shipp, or from the belongings of the company,' He repeats that Croker 'waifted the shipp to the harbor north of Garrachigo, and also gave the scotts a drabler and bonnet.' The incident closes in a counterfeit glow of friendship; one is reminded of the exasperated foreigner's comment on some native customs: 'After exchanging two or three stabs with a knife, even when they wound each other, they will make peace instantly, and go away and drink together.' It passes belief that the Scots, paying their reluctant call on the *Reprisal*, were not offered drinks, and lavish drinks at that.

THE DIRTY DEALER

By way of contrast with Croker, who was a tough customer but capable of compunction and second thoughts—even though they primarily concerned his own safety—we have here a specimen unrelievedly nasty, who preyed on people not only helpless, but

* HCA 13–34, reverse of p. 181, unnumbered

totally unable to formulate any sort of resistance or self-protection. He could plunder them again and again with impunity, and there can be little doubt that he did so; pirate is too good a word for him. Since his technique of thievery seems foolproof, owing to its remote locations and the inability of the plundered to give evidence, one is especially glad to see that the Admiralty Court got its hands on him, and even more hopeful of a final engagement in Wapping or Southwark.

When the character and testimony of John Adey* first dawn on our admiring sight (25 August 1600) he is commander of the *Cordelia* of London, a fairly small ship apparently, for she is also called 'a barquete. In wch,' he informs us, 'there was an hundreth and thirty negroes, and noe other goodes.'

This terrible freight—crammed into the hold of the little ship, unsupplied with food, water or air—had been stolen bodily from a plantation 'nere Buta, in the Island of the Barbathos.' Not that the plantation was any health cure assuredly, but at least the slaves had some minimum expectation of eating, drinking and breathing. Having made his capture, Adey started to treat with the owner, an unnamed 'portingall from Moro' on his conditions for returning them. The owner was highly interested in getting his property back, of course, and in return 'delyvered to him for them, certaine pearle to the quantity of fower score ounces.'

This transaction seems to have been not only satisfactory to Adey, but gave him such a bright idea that he set sail for another promising location.

'From Moro he wente unto Ryo de Gatcha, where he founde severall pearle boates, one of wch he and his company broke upp for fire woode. And he resting there and threateninge the people that they should make no viadge [pearl fishing] with the sd boates, they gave him one Bullion of sylver and goulde, to the valew of one hundreth poundes or there aboute.' Having received his blackmail money he sailed away 'and,' he concludes, innocently wide-eyed, 'he and his company tooke no other goodes during his last viadge.'

Unfortunately for him the next witness, 'Beniamyn Watkyn of Ratcliffe' throws the usual extra light on some episodes that Adey has carefully forgotten. He confirms the sale of the

* HCA 13–34—p. 331 reverse

Negroes for pearls, but mentions an additional sale of slaves 'at the Island of the West Indies called Margarita, to a factor or owner.' In his account of the pearl-fishery at Rio de Gatcha, he reveals that 'they chased fyve or six pearle boates wch sunke them selves'; Adey has said they chased one and broke it up. He testifies that the bribe to go away—the bullion—weighed about a hundred and fifty pounds; Adey has cooled this down to a hundred. The thought that this offering might have been scraped up among the pearl fishers themselves is a painful one; at least there has been no mention of any owner or employer contributing. He recalls the rifling of 'a Barque laded with Spanish and Portingall ales' which Adey has omitted to mention, also 'a friggott wch they chased, but it had not any goodes, money, pearles, Jewells or other things of accompte.' He signs his deposition in good writing, and is backed up by the last examinate, John Brouse, who confirms the last witness pretty generally except that Watkyn has been silent (or perhaps genuinely forgetful) of the final item, the frigate: this it seems was searched unmercifully, and some 'Jares [jars] of wyne and other victuals' stolen from it. When any of this lot from Adey down said that a ship had nothing valuable in it, they knew what they were talking about.

XV
Local Voices

Hundreds of small cargo ships must have moored in the Thames, day in day out. If accidents happened to them, as they frequently did, they must have meant genuine hardship to owners and their employees alike, in default (as has been said) of insurances or any other protection. The fact that the present case got before the Admiralty Court means that the winner collected damages, perhaps, but nothing survives to show one way or the other. What does survive is the pleasant name of the ship, also the voice of a young man (name illegible) giving evidence with an occasional and unconscious felicity of phrase.*

'The *Darling* was at anchor in the Thames,' he testifies, 'and betwixt 2 and 3 of the clocke in the morninge, the *Gamaliell* nexte to the *Darling* came foule of her and thwearte [athwart] of her hawlse. And drew her ankers and carried her to the south of the water.'

The young man, who must have been left aboard as night watchman, was roused from sleep 'by a greate crackinge betwixt them. And fearinge greate hurte was don, this d^te called up Mr Hiscocke, and told him that his ship was out of her moorings and brought on the other side of the water.'

Mr Hiscocke, the owner, must have lived somewhere nearby. With understandable consternation 'he called a boate': the river, like London, apparently never slept. Having got the boat immediately, 'he wente on borde his shippe and brought her again into her moorings.'

The watchman now describes the damages—severe enough, especially as the *Darling* was already under repair. 'A stage [scaffolding] on the shippe, made for the men to worke on, was broken downe by the *Gamaliell*, and some decke boardes that lay on the stage were lost, and nothing lefte but 2 planckes,' he continues. 'And 2 Railes on the poope of the *Darling* were broken, and also a Spritt saile yard, and one of the sterne postes

* HCA 13–42—p. 53

broken, wch were already repaired and amended excepte the hiclines [guard rope?] wch are not yet don.'

At least, however, they had a responsible man to deal with. 'Nexte morninge being Sunday, Mr Hiscocke hired Sandys men to iudge what yt would cost to repaire the same, wch they estimated; and he putt it under their handes.' But trouble was on the way, as often happens with a first estimate. The boatyard owner 'said yt would cost the sd Hiscocke more moneys than are severally sett downe in the [first] skedle; for Mr Sandys is a shipps carpenter and is well acquainted with the same.'

It is this increase of the estimate, apparently, that has brought the two ship owners into Court; the Examinations are full of beautiful rows about contracts for ship repairs, at which there is no time even to glance.

Now Thomas Clerk, also of the *Darling*, contributes some details rather comfortless for the *Gamaliel*. 'When the *Gamaliell* first ankered beside the *Darling*,' he testifies, 'this ex^{ate} advised them of the *Gamaliell* to anker further off, for feare of wronge wch one shipp might doe to the other.' This request the *Gamaliel* ignored, not only with the results we have seen but with an earlier collision, not yet referred to.

'In the night tyme, upon the flud,' Clerk continues, 'she came uppon the *Darling* and brake downe her wales on the poope. And on the 4th day of April' came the second, more serious accident.

Now the first witness is recalled, apparently on some contention by the defendants that darkness or the tide was responsible.

'Yt was very fine wether, and a light moone shine,' he repudiates the argument, 'and the tides was then at the full. The *Darling*,' he adds affectionately, 'was lighte in her ballaste, and floted upp and downe' before the *Gamaliel* took the heart out of her.

Surely the *Gamaliel*'s owners had to cough up; after two warnings, they had taken not an ounce of precaution. One relies on the commodity dispensed by the Admiralty Court, which was justice.

Loose talk in Wapping

The chief staple of gossip in Wapping—apart from hangings—must have been doings aboard ship. Many seamen originated here, and those who did not would linger in the pubs of this Thames-side port and exchange uninhibited memories of the voyage. Wapping and Southwark both would have been ringing, before long, with any casualty, any dispute, misfortune, crime or scandal that had happened on the way home.

The present instance,* though mostly concerned with a juicy female character who kept an alehouse, originated aboard ship. The sparking point was a case of alleged theft among the company; the loot changes bewilderingly from witness to witness, but at last settles down to a clutch of silver coins and—very belatedly—to a gold chain likewise. Who is lying, remains a mystery; no one could steer a clear course in this welter of contradictions, poor memories, and the confusion natural to uneducated people who can hardly marshal their thoughts for the purpose of sustained narrative.

The trouble began when their ship, the *True Love*, sighted a vessel bearing toward them that looked uncommonly like a pirate. This was followed by the company's usual rush to conceal any valuables; for this purpose the ship's carpenter had long since made 'a secrett hole in the sd shipp', and was just closing it up again when the trouble begins with the testimony of one Thomas Taylor. He had found a glove; by his account, just an ordinary glove. 'He shewed it to Colthurst the mʳ, saying, Master, you have lefte something in the Cooke roome. And the sd Colthurst answered, saying, I pray thee, run downe and shove yt betwyxt the decks, where the rest of the money [sic] is. And thereuppon,' Taylor continues, 'he went betwyxt the decks, and seeing the carpenter making upp [closing up] the hole, said , Hold brother, hold, I have a thinge to putt in. And so the sd Taylor putt the glove and that wch was yn yt [something not mentioned before] into the sd hole. And the carpenter asked the sd Taylor, What ys yt, and he answered, I think brother, yt ys a glove with Rialles' [reales].

Here the testimony diverges; we find that the distant sail was not a pirate after all. The hole was reopened, and the glove

* HCA 13–42—pp. 102–6

proved to be missing. Thomas German, one of the crew, in testimony offers his opinion: 'that yf the sd glove had fallen downe to the bottom of the shipp, yt would not be taken out until the shipp had been valude' [valued]. Meanwhile Taylor is strenuously declaring his innocence: 'He putt the glove in the hole as he claymed to doe. And if any say he did not they depose falsely. ffor this dpte hath as witnesses John Needham and Moyses Grapewell, who were sitting by the pumpe betwyxt the deckes, drinking tobacco* [sic] when the sd Taylor putt the glove in the hole.' Needham supports him: 'He knoweth yt to be true, ffor that this d^{pte} was hard by, drinking of tobacco with the sd Moyses.'

Of course the ship, by the time it had docked at Wapping, was bursting with the ill-will of the opposing opinions and argument that landed the contenders in the Admiralty Court. This is where we have the good fortune to meet Mistress Elizabeth Wilkinson, 'uxor Jacobi Wilkinson de Wappinge', and keeper of the alehouse mentioned.†

'The late Robert Colthurst, aboute a weeke before he wente to Senlege [St Leger?]', she deposes with spirit, 'came to her house in company with William Dyckman, and called for beere.'

(Interpreting 'late' in its usual meaning: has Colthurst died recently? This point is never cleared up.)

'And as he was talkinge and drinkinge,' she pursues, 'they fell in talke of a chaine of gould that was gon [disappeared] in Colthurst's shipp.'

This is the first appearance, after all this time, of the chain. Dyckman now makes a first-class blunder.

'The sd Dyckman, beinge very much in drinke before he came thither,' Elizabeth recounts, 'said the boatswaine, as he thought, had the sd chaine. And at the same instant, the boatswaine's wife came into the house', just in time to hear him. The unpleasantness was now off to a good start. Appealing to Colthurst, the woman 'wept, sayinge her husband was as cleare of the same as a child unborne.'

Colthurst, in obvious consternation, could not detach himself from Dyckman quickly enough.

---

* This seems to be sailors' contemporary talk; the expression seems unknown to maritime experts on the period.

† HCA 13–42—p. 106

'He prayed her to be quiett, sayinge, I pray God the Divell take me body and soule, if I thinke that thy husband hath the chaine.'

After this appeal to both addresses at once the wretched Dyckman made some attempt to deny what he had said, but Elizabeth ploughed him under on a couple of counts. 'This d^pte being present held him to his words. And she knoweth that William Dyckman is a man much given to drinke, and is so week in braine that a suppe or two of drinke will over throwe him. And that he is very often drunk, and for such is knowen amongst his neighbors.'

In the brief Interrogatory, Elizabeth comes out well. 'She hath lived in Wappinge about XVI years; she favoreth [one defendant] no more than the other, and wisheth that right may take place.' When asked for details of her property she answers 'that her husband is at Sea, and hath a greate parte thereof with him', and therefore she cannot oblige. Then she identifies a few others who were present at the alehouse fracas: 'Peter Parrye whom she hath knowen for aboute XVI years, and never hearde but what he was an honest man': others she describes as 'such psons as would not talke falsely or depose untrewly.'

Heretofore she has spoken with the caution and reserve of a businesswoman unwilling to antagonize her customers; but now —apparently—bitterness overcomes her. The whole thing is Dyckman's fault; by his imbecile carelessness of speech he has landed them all in the Admiralty Court, and she really gets down to swinging the axe. 'She knoweth him as a week brayned fellowe often overseene in drinke,' she repeats furiously, yet her automatic caution so far catches up that she adds somewhat lamely, 'He wrongeth him selfe more than any other she knoweth.' She refers to her house as 'a victualling house' rather than a drinking ditto, and having stood nobly by all her clients— always excepting Dyckman—she signs herself EW, the letters uneven but not ill-formed.

As to the nature of this case: by competent authority the Admiralty Court did not try libel cases, yet this one—with its minute questioning on who said what about whom—seems to be nothing else. By all appearance, the boatswain and his wife were suing Dyckman; not for any question of damages, for the defendant was poor as well as worthless, but solely for the protection of their good name—in a word, public vindication from the stigma of thief.

If only the Examinations had been held in public instead of in strict privacy: Elizabeth is really Mistress Quickly, with a sharper edge. Again, what a character for Shakespeare.

ANNOYING THE THAMES

The regulations here quoted* are of April 1604. Their chief characteristic seems to be that no sooner formulated than violated; the lists of such offences are endless.

'ffor throwinge dunge and filth, to the greate annoyance of the River of Thames'; 'ffor annoyinge the Thames with filth and rubbishe oute of his docke'; 'ffor annoying the River of Thames with weedes falling from off his wharfe'. This last seems very mild, but the transgressions quickly pick up steam. 'Thomas Daves of the Cooke [Cock] and bull at ye demitagg hoy [?], for casting filth thereon from a house of offis, in the Thames; for having a Leystall of dunge and filth, and at the flowing of the tide the filth is borne away by the water, to the greate annoyance of the River of Thames'; 'John Matley of London Bridge, for throwinge Dust into the Thames out of his house.'

The hurt feelings of the river were fairly well matched by the sensibilities of docks and steps:

'ffor annoying the Armitage docke by the unloading of Sande; for the throwinge of ashes, to the greate hurt of the sd docke': 'Peeter Leonard, for not repayring his wharfe, and rubbige falling into ye Thames'; 'ye Tallow Chandlers for defacing a payer of Comon Steyres [pair of common stairs] at St Ollofes Watergate, to the great hinderrance of the Kinges Leege peepell.' No doubt these slovenly characters—whose breed continues among us undiminished, but confined to chewing gum wrappers and metal pulls off beer cans—were fined; the more severely, the better. Against Thomas Kempe—by way of ending —stands the accusation of 'a Pickled herringe', never elucidated; with this cryptic image the imagination, unconfined, may toy at its leisure.

* HCA 1–6—pp. 76 and 106

XVI
A Mystery

Crime is a word we have seen applied to piracy, in a dozen contexts. Merely being one of a pirate company was a crime; pillage of goods was a crime; menacing and abusing their victims was a crime; above all, killing others during the attack on a ship—whether by shot, sword, dagger or bludgeon—was a crime which the indictment called murder, and undoubtedly it was murder considering the attendant circumstances. But there is another species of murder separate and apart, unconnected with combat or violence of any kind, loathed by (at least) some of the very men who would cheerfully cut down an opponent: the crime of murder by poison, the method steeped in infamy from its origins in darkness to its victims in agony—agony which sometimes, in the case of arsenic especially, could simulate a genuine illness.

References to poisoning in the Admiralty Court papers cannot be called frequent, yet they are there. A superficial and scattering survey such as the present one cannot turn up the mathematical proportion; they seem to occur, say, as one case among thousands. A remarkable example is that of Edward ffold, 1606,* a notorious pirate whose indictment ranges steadily through five counts of routine offences against different ships; the number of witnesses who testify against him—fourteen of them—suggest that they had been biding their time to get back at him. Then suddenly the indictment changes colour with: 'for killinge Tom Andrewes on borde the *hopewell*', and mounts to a climax: 'ffor poysoninge Mr Thompson on borde the *Mistres*'. Not only are both murders sworn to by a total of four witnesses, but ffold himself—probably exhausted by questioning—has confessed the first one, and the second is 'partly proved by the oathes of John Hawkins, Thomas Hurrey and Adam Fowler.' In a much later example of 19 December 1676,† 'Hugh Davies has poisoned Simon Cumberland and

* HCA 1–5—no. 33   † HCA 1–10/106

killed John Harmon, both in the *Samuel and Henry*.' Again the
repetition of the earlier pattern: the habitual killer who strikes
down or poisons, whichever is most convenient. The fate of ffold
and Davies is unlocatable, but what with their own confessions,
is surely beyond doubt.

But the final example is a genuine mystery, beginning—like
the crime itself—in darkness, and also ending there. This bit of
torn paper, of very poor and fragile quality, fell out of volume
HCA 13-34 (Examinations); either a second sheet or the
lower half of a first. A considerable search has failed to locate
the crime of which it speaks. Not a single name is mentioned in
it, not the victim's, the criminal's, not that of the ship in which
it happened. The awful script, general phraseology and broken
narrative indicate a person largely uneducated but who was—
all the same—not too stupid, and who could moreover write.
One guess as to its provenance, which may be accepted or
rejected as one likes, is that the writer (almost certainly a
woman) spoke a country dialect that could not be understood by
the examining Judge, and was requested to put her evidence in
writing. This terrible record is given whole and entire, except
for small deletions where meanings are either incomprehensible,
or (more likely) the unaccustomed labour of writing has
produced in the writer a momentary daze.

'. . . and when he was sseck [sick] his body was waistt
[wasted] and clene, and being but one hower dead he did swill
[swell] and cam black, that the woman [the witness?] did
razone he was poysoned. this examinat dooth know the yong
man ssprached off [spoke of] the cook, and did not lyv ffyve
dayes after. they hoof [have] one day give him freshe meate.
And he did not sslepe in all thys tim, but was in most various
tourment, and was ssodyn [suddenly] sseck.'

There follows a completely garbled sentence indicating that
the 'yong man' begged to speak to the cook: 'but styll cook he
cayred not, he would not com to clean him, himselff beinge
comanded by Jons, by boot [both] Spyker and the pilott and
dyvars [diverse] off the company to com to him, but he would
not. And Dan fforbes being in the ship, this cook would get him
away [take him to one side?] and speke to him. And he [Dan]
went away, he [the cook] made him. soe he wld doe iff guiltye.
And at his ffysrt meat [the first meal aboard, evidently] this

adams herde the yong mans sspeche agaynst the cook. this was his farest [first] meat. And he did some tow [two] tymes fall, and the cook sayd he had the ffalling ssickness, which is most untoore [untoward; unlikely]. And his head was cut to the beare scolle [bare skull]. And he was clear [sensible], and ssome one did hear all his Sspeaches, being one that did wacks [watch] with him booth day and nyght, [herself?], and did sse him make quars [quarrels] with the cook abord the shipe, and was all wayes pykin quarrell [picking quarrels] agaynst him.' (No signature, date, or other sign of origin.)

In this record straight from hell, there remains the consolation that the case was before the Admiralty Court, that ruthless sifter of secrets. Whether the poisoning was the case itself or only subsidiary to a principal case we cannot know, but at least it had come to light during the proceedings. Was the cook already in custody? If not, surely the hunt for him was up. His indifference to suffering is reminiscent of Mrs Turner, industrious poisoner to the Countess of Essex, who tried out nitric acid on a cat, 'wherewith the cat languished and pitifully cried for the space of 2 days, and then died'. There exist a few people for whom *peine forte et dure* seems made exactly to order. In all this uncertainty there remains to us one certain vision: the cook, probably in the best of good humours, bringing the young man his food, delicately touched up with arsenic.

XVII
Allsorts

In this roaring legal welter of conflicts, antagonisms and abuse, of cruelty and murder in four or five languages, there are invariably found notes minor and disconnected; not having any important bearing upon the cause in hand perhaps, yet in their stray gleams reflecting who knows what circumstances of life and secrets of personality, of imagination, of malice open or covert. But language, the key to the inner man or woman, changes its shape considerably with every century. Expressions common in their day are lost beyond recovery in a few hundred years—not a long time in historical terms—and we are left with conjecture, but entertaining conjecture. Or where the terms have not lost validity but are perfectly plain to us, what remains is the pleasure of *evidence*; the lies and the honesties both that make the people who spoke that evidence come alive to us.

The documentary language of the Court, as has been mentioned, was exclusively Latin, but not the classical Latin of schools. This legal species is often a sight to behold when the stenographer's vocabulary runs out and he is forced to invent equivalent words and terminations, or to relapse into English. Sometimes the look of these invented forms so alarms him that he feels compelled to follow them up with a translation: 'pisces Anglice nuncupatos shrympes'; 'duodecias cockiara, twentie spoones of mother of pearle', and 'unam Cimbam vocatam a Corke boate'. The formula, *they comforted and maintained*, becomes 'comfortarunt et maintenarunt', and others appear where shipments, say of ordinary household wares, drive the writer first into strange looking Latin, then back in desperation upon English. When a small piracy takes place in the Thames, an unknown scribe puts his whole heart into the jurors' writ: 'tres pisces salsas thre salte fishe, parvas funes smale roapes', and ends the formulary 'against the peace' etc, with an indignant

'!' Exclamation marks are so non-existent in documents of this sort, that one cannot help parading a lone specimen; also it is nice to see that the writer feels so strongly about it.

The feeling for language, in other aspects, is found in the names of ships. Surely the man who named his ship *Fat Swine* (of Ostend) was moved by some sardonic fancy? A jaunty challenge seems to ring in the *Why Not*, never jauntier than when her crew were busy pillaging 'from a shipp, four large sackes of spanishe money to the valew of V hundred poundes English.' *Blacke Balbiana* seems to cast a shadow and *Blue Worme* a charnel smell, but *Little Bess* is affectionate and *Jesus of Rye* sounds trustful; sad that such childlike faith failed to keep her out of the Admiralty Court. One or two names, however, seem astonishingly modern for the early seventeenth century, a cargo ship named *Transporter*, for instance, while *Wagon* sounds rustic and hardworking.

Although (strictly speaking) proper names are not language, yet the effect of more grotesque specimens reflect a stage of the language itself—which was not really tamed, we remember, till late in the eighteenth century. John Fidge, John Pretious, Jeffery Poote; Thomas Gutter, Daniel Giggle and Wicked Davy are fair examples; the Dutch bring up the rear not ingloriously with Conradus Heckleberche, Abraham Laus and Humfridus Grubb. What torment John Pretious must have endured in today's English schools. By the way, one Peter Christmas* is accused of piracy (1591) but let out on bail. 'Christmas' is a most uncommon surname; could this miscreant have been grandfather or great-grandfather to Charles I's three great Carvers to the Navy, Garrard, John and Matthias Christmas?

Also by the way—faintly so, but there—runs a gaggle of witless graffiti scrawled on the endpapers of the Examinations themselves. These are always in English and are, one would guess, the product of moments of bored but justifiable inattention: moments, say, when a judge was trying to pound the meaning of a question into some thick skull and the stenographer could share his instant of leisure with some kindred spirit sitting nearby. Speak they dared not while the inquisition was going

* HCA 3/176

forward, but stray idiocies on the flyleaf were not beyond their power. One man even breaks into verse:

> 'I marvell much what wise men mene
> to love woman soe well,
> which knows it is the only spoil
> that hee doth not sell.'

His own creation? Bad enough, at any rate, to make his friend object: 'Roger! your writinge is to [too] good for myne. Soe be yt'—a dialogue which still echoes, faintly, with the guffaws (stifled) of feebleminded amusement.

RAYSINS

These humble accessories of puddings, cakes and pies have never before attained to such heights of literary prominence; or to put it another way, never were raisins gone bad dealt with at such length. Wherever the eye lights during the Examination it meets the word, spelled differently each time, and each time sounding a different note of threnody, all dated 15 January 1600.* Who is suing who, in this case, does not come out clearly till later. Here John Pemberton is testifying against Robert Cobb, William Harrison and Frauncis Taylor, merchants:

'About Aprill laste paste, this ex^ate had sighte of aboute fower hundreth pecces [containers] of Mallaga raysins in a ware house, wch were the goodes of the sd Cobb, Harrison and Taylor. And yf the reasins wch this ex^ate sawe had beene drye and well conditioned, they had beene worthe at the least nineteene shillings the hundreth weighte; wch he knoweth to be true, because he hath boughte them him selfe, and sawe others buy at that tyme such well conditioned and drye at that prize [price] and rate. But these raysons were soe wette and evill conditioned with salte water, or freshe, or both, this ex^ate broocke of [broke off] with the merchants, and would not have them att eighte shillings and IIIId the hundreth.'

Then for some unknown reason, after this dismal sight, Pemberton did buy 'the first fower peeces of Reasins for eighte shillings the hundreth weighte', but hastens to assert that they

HCA 34—p. 418

were no better than the rest: 'so befouled they were in a very
evill sorte. And the plaintiff, by the fower hundereth peeces of
reasins, sustayned losse, nyne or teen [ten] shillings in the
hundereth wheite.'

Why did he buy them, one may ask? Whatever the answer,
the Interrogatory is now upon him; first he makes the obscure
and baffling announcement that 'he comes to speake the truthe
in this cause, at the requeste of Mr Harrison', and after this
declines to give any account of his means: 'As for his Estate, he
believeth he is not bounde to reveale the same.' These pre-
liminaries done with, he returns to his cut-rate purchase: 'The
raysins were not rotten, but soe wette that some of them might
have byne wronge [wrung]. And the wett rose from them and
stoode on the floure [floor] under them; neither did he ever see
in his life tyme such a parcel of raysins soe wett and evill
smelled.'

Now John Woodwarde, an associate of Pemberton's, adds
his bit with a few new notes: 'By the procurement [solicitation]
of the sd merchants, he sawe in a ware house in Jeames Streate,
IIII peeces or frayles of Mallaga reasons; and all or moste
parte of them were soe wette that the water runne from them
where they laye. And he tasted some of them, and they were
soe salte that they stuncke, and were all most rotten.' He, unlike
Pemberton, does not resist giving his financial status: 'He is
worth 500l, his debtes being payd; he is settled [registered?
enrolled?] to her Ma^ty at ten hundereth. And he cometh to
speake a truthe in this cause at the request of the plaintiffs, and
at their chardges if any bee.'

During some further discourse it is not the plaintiff, defendants or witnesses who begin to founder, but the unfortunate
man who must take all this down; the mere sound of raisins—by
this time—has addled his wits and driven his spelling to a new
low. 'The moste parte of the rasens were weett, troden uppon
and tossed to and froe, as it seamed.'

F IGGS AND W YNE

A very brief postscript might be added here; not on any
biographical or emotional aspect in the life of the fig, but in
order to illustrate the very strict surveillance, aboard ship, in

accepting cargo. The *Greyhound* of London, lading at Brazil (1612) was to take on an unspecified quantity of figs. 'And when the figgs were brought on borde by one Cortes, the tapnetts were not full, to the number of twenty. And the m^r founde faulte therewith, and would not receave them on borde.'

Worse was on its way.

'And at the lading of the sd forty pipes of wyne, some of the company p'ceaved that the butts were not full, and called the Cowper [deliverer of the shipment] who found that the butt wanted elleven ynches of full. And the Cowper promised to bring a barrell of wyne on borde to fill up the same, but he brought not any.' Undoubtedly the receivers of the cargo must have made difficulties over the crooked supplier's bill, and who can blame them? In any case figgs and wyne, no less than raysins, echo and re-echo through three folio pages, closely written. Somehow this meticulous inspection of lading, early in the seventeenth century, takes one by surprise.

XVIII
Letters of Reprisal

These Letters are all interesting, but chiefly in an unexpected direction—as betraying personal characteristics of the monarch under whom they were formulated. One such document* issued 1585 is a little extraordinary in beginning as a regulation official document: 'Whereas our Sovereigne Lady Elizabeth Queene of England being credibly [informed] that the King of Spaine hath made stay of the shipps and goodes of her loving subjects', but ending as a personal licence to one man, Robert Kitchin, 'to take the goods of the subjects of the King of Spaine, wheresoever upon the seas.' Kitchin, 'merchant of Bristowe, hath made proof before me that his losses do amount to the sume of 6500 £. And he hath equipped one shipp called the *Gift of God*, 150 tons, with 80 mariners and men of war, with 24 cast pieces and fowlers of iron, which is authorized to set upon and take by force of arms, any ship or goods of the subjects of the King of Spaine.'

The Letter then moves on to what one feels is the chief clause of any Elizabethan Letter of Reprisal—the obligation of the owner, having captured a prize or prizes, 'not to break bulk before a true inventory be taken thereof, and an appraisement be made of the said goodes.' Here is the Queen's great object, her determination to get her cut of anything valuable, arising from her unsleeping (and justifiable) preoccupation with money. The virtual bankruptcy of the England which Mary delivered into her hands—ruined commerce, partly from activity of pirates—was a lesson never forgotten. This particular Letter is signed not by Elizabeth but by her Lord Admiral, Charles Howard.

The following communication, 7 April 1628,† ringing with the urgent necessity for combating the same horrors under Charles I, is from Lord High Admiral Buckingham to 'my very Lovinge frend Sr Henry Marden K^t, Judge of the High Courte of

* HCA 13–34—p. 243   † HCA 13–34—p. 224

Admiraltie.' It sets up a preliminary machinery on behalf of
'such of his Ma^{ts} Subiects as have sustained hurte, losse or
damage' through piracy; the offenders mentioned are Spain, the
States General of the Dutch Provinces, and—just to leave
nobody out—'Subiects of the King of Spaine inhabiting in the
Lowe Countries.' The procedure is laid down: those who have
suffered loss by piracy are to register details on oath at the
Admiralty ,'that I may give you p'ticular Order for the graunting
of Comissions of Marque and Reprisall according to his Ma^{ts}
pleasure.'

Buckingham receives later a highly specific letter from the
Judges of the Admiralty, on behalf of 'Captaine Lewis Kerke
mercer, a naturell Subiect of the King of England, conveying
the *Ghoste* bounde for London, was taken by Dunkerkers,
stript to his Shirte, rifled of One hundred and Twelve pounds
Sterl money and other goods to the value of 200l Sterl, and
carried prisoner to Dunkerke.' Here the Captain 'ransomed
himselfe, together with the charges of his imprisonment [the
gall], wch cost him Twoe hundered and threscore pounds Sterl.'
If he is petitioning for a Letter of Reprisal, he probably got it;
he is spoiling for revenge, and no wonder.

The same battle against the hydra, beginning without loss of
time on 2 November 1625, continues with 'the Kings Comission
for Comissions of Reprizall.'* The document is as long as
admirable; after the customary statement that 'many of our
lovinge Subjects have sustained Divers and Sundry great
Wronge, Losses and damages at Sea' it sets out the remedy as
well as the conditions pertaining thereto, which may be
summarized briefly:

1. Whereas the formes of Princes and States in amity have
bin observed and Used in Seekinge restitution for the said
losses and Damages, and yet noe restitucon can be obteined:
2. And whereas our Subiects have made Suite unto us for
letters of Reprizall, they having noe other means for
Justice [except] to take the Shippes and goods of the sd
King of Spaine or his Subiects uppon the Seas, or in any
port in his possession:
3. Wee have thought fitt, with the advice of our privy

* HCA 25-224

Councell, that letters of Reprizall shalbe graunted to those persons who have suffered Losses, and whoe shall desire the same.

4. Therefore these are to require and authorize you as our High Admirall, to graunte your Comissions for takeing of the shipps and marchandice of the sd King of Spaine or his Subiects, to such of our Subiects soe Dampnified, or to bee Dampnified hereafter.

Having laid down the grounds of permission, the document goes on to make clear—in utmost detail—the restrictions of such permission.

5. That all desireinge such Letters of Reprizall, shall first make proofe or informacon before the Judge of the Admiraltie, that their losses have byn such as they pretende [claim] to have susteyned.

Then, very importantly if familiarly:

6. The sd merchants shall give bonde at the Admiraltie, *that they shall bringe such* Shippes and goodes wch they shall take, to *some porte of his Ma^{ts} realme.*

Now a provision as tough as anguish-making:

7. That all such shippes and goodes shalbe kepte in safety, and noe parte of them solde, spoiled, wasted or diminished, untill Judgm^t hath byn passed in the High Courte of Admiraltie, that the sd goodes are lawfull prize; *otherwise the sd Comission shalbe voyde, as well to the taker as to others that shall buy the sd goodes or medle with them.*

In the next, every remaining hole is stopped up:

8. That yf there be necessitie to sell goodes that be periture [perishable]: in this case the Judge of Admiraltie shall graunte p'mission to take an Inventory thereof, by five honest and Sufficient men, and sell the same; and to returne the proceed into the Courte of Admiraltie: there to remaine untill it is decided, to whom they shall appertaine.'

Someone is always taking the joy out of life. However, once the judgment is in their favour, the winners 'may make sale in open markett, or howsoever ells to thier best advantage; to enjoy the same as lawfull prize, and as their owne proper goodes.

And it shalbe lawfull for other persons to buy of the sd goodes without any trouble, molestacon or incumbrance, as if the sd goodes had byn come by through Lawfull Traffique.'

There follows a list of Commissions of Reprisal granted from 15 November 1625, to 25 March 1628, sum total 240, or about 80 per annum. All of them are granted in the name of 'George Duke of Buckingham: to all Christian people, Greetinge in our Lord God everlasting.' At this point* the book of Commissions comes to a close; to one person it is moving that the next tattered volume in the series† opens with the poignant note: 'All the Comissions followinge were graunted post mortem Ducis Buckinghamiae.' Now it is Charles himself who makes a declaration of familiar form, but written to a new address—the French King's—for Letters of Reprisal against him; he signs it, 'Witness O Selfe, in the 12the yeare of O Raigne.' This is dated 30 September 1628 and is also signed by fourteen of the Privy Council, as well as by the superb Thomas Coventry, builder (with Charles I and Pepys) of the English Navy. Again there follow up to 1629 Letters granted to thirty ships, some of whose names are evocative: *Dayntee Delight*, *Comforte*, *Bride*, *Charity* and *Swanne*; other names perhaps the oncoming darkness: *Job* and *Pilgryme*.

One more reference must be made to a declaration by Charles in 1637 which seems (again to one person) to embody that quality of humanity that, in spite of disheartening experience, in him seemed with passing years to grow greater instead of less. His words are equalled by Howard's after the Armada, but Howard was speaking on behalf of his countrymen. Has any other ruler, contemporary with Charles I, spoken so on behalf of foreigners, technically enemy foreigners at that? First of all, while stiffening the regulations for bringing in prizes and not breaking bulk, the King is anxious to have it understood that 'the Lʳˢ of Reprizall nowe yelded to some of his Maᵗˢ subiects are but soe many temporary dispensacons, and necessarily aforded from his Maᵗʸ, for a Supply of that Justice which hath byn wantinge from the ffrench Kinge.'

Then, having spoken at the prompting of his troubled and scrupulous conscience, he strikes the note seldom heard in his merciless century, full of an unaccustomed music:

* HCA 24   † HCA 25

'Noe violence shalbe don to the persons of the ffrench subiects, excepte in case of resistance. And after [their] blood hath byn spilled, *the hurte or wounded shalbe used with all convenient offices of humanity and kindnes.*'

XIX
The Gap

On 5 July 1640 a man named John Walpole, 'on borde his M^{ats} ship the *Guard-land*', submitted to authority a list of observations spoken by his shipmates, all of disloyalty flagrant enough to qualify as rebellion, and all of them black arrows pointing to future disaster.* Precisely to what Naval department he offered this is unknown, but it made its way into the Examinations and stands there, unqualified and unexplained.

'July 25, 1639: Thomas Cooke the Boatswaine did say, that King Charles was a Tyrant in demanding Ship-monies, and that in England kinges had beene deposed and murdered for lesse matters; and for instifying [giving instances of] his speeches, the deposing of Kinge Richard the second of England, and Jehu's killing of Jehoram.' John has his witnesses to this neatly lined up: himself, William Peperall Chirurgion, and Enoch Bostocke.

28 July 1639: 'William Soames, Corporall of the ship, did say that these pamphletts cast abroad by the Scotts against the King was very truthe', and so forth.

Ship Money is a reference especially pregnant. This very moderate impost in support of the Navy was initiated in 1634 by Charles, who was driven to the measure by the desperate state of his ships, and only after his own rigid search for precedents—going back before 1066—had confirmed his right to levy it. The instant response of the whole kingdom to this—from covert resistances and evasions to riots and violences offered the collectors—had risen by 1640 to a universal uproar that forced the King to relinquish the tax. This account leads us directly back to Walpole the informer, a character never very well regarded—and yet his efforts seem amateurish compared to the flood of neighbourhood betrayers and tattlers in response to the State's inducement of 1649: 'Those who inform on traitors to the Commonwealth will have for their pains, part of such traitors' estates.'

* HCA 1–7—p. 144

All this is by way of demonstrating the gap that has opened between the King and his subjects. Still another one festers beneath the surface—the splits and cracks in the population's sympathies, defined later by a Lt Horsemondon: 'One third are implacable enemies [to the King], a third are cold and a third are loyal.' This in turn has brought us to the summer of 1640; in a few more years opens the ruinous period 1646–9. And strangely enough these first two gaps—of sympathy—are matched by a third, the gap in documentary evidence; a (seemingly) total disappearance of records of the Admiralty Court. True that other massive disappearances are not unknown, for example a huge quantity of Naval papers under Charles II. Yet this last is explained, first by the Naval Offices 'being lately burnt out of ye Navy Office', and second by the epidemic of plague that forced the Navy Office to move out of town. The plague of Civil War, perhaps, drove our missing documents into oblivion.

And during this interval, what has happened to the pirate? If to this question no absolutely definite answer appears, certain guides exist whose indications might be followed cautiously. In 1624 Charles I inherited, as has been said, a Navy too ruinous to protect his eroded commerce and open coasts preyed on by hosts of such parasites, some of them cosily ensconced on small islands offshore. In a mere ten years—by 1634—the number of piracy cases has greatly diminished; to whom can we ascribe this but to the King, tireless rebuilder and supporter of the Navy? Yet in the same year, 1634, begins this enormous documentary gap not only in the records of the Admiralty Court, but also in that awesome compendium called the Calendar of State Papers Domestic. An overhauling of the Calendar for this disturbed period produces few allusions to piracy or piracy trials, while in volumes of other series—some relating exclusively to piracy—the vacuum is similar. The last entry in HCA 25 of 4 April 1637, skips to an entry of 25 June 1649 which is a general declaration against piracy, signed by Joseph Bradshawe. The following entry—for Letters of Reprisal, headed 'Keepers of the Liberty of England'—is a tacit admission of the continuing existence of pirates; it is signed by an illiterate hand which may or may not be John Giddins.

XX

Presente: the Kinges most Excelente Majestie

With the above words begin about four-fifths of Council meetings relating to the Navy. Charles was present on all such occasions where business of importance was on the agenda, even if some stenographers chop down the formula to *Present: King*. His absences were invariably when procedure was routine and could be left entirely in the hands of his Council—of whom two at least were outstanding and a third and fourth (Pepys and Coventry, of course) were equal at least to any advisory body under the sun.

The King's Navy was the great hunter and taker of pirates. Not invariably, of course; we shall see astonishing self-defence by small merchant ships, but the Navy was essentially the scourer of seas, the bulwark against depredation of England's commerce, fisheries and collieries.

As much as his father had done Charles II loved the Navy, and his love was reinforced by his extensive knowledge of ships and of maritime warfare, and his professional skill as a pilot. Any consecutive reading of his Councils with particular reference to naval affairs must increase—must constantly heighten —the sense of his quality, of his unassuming expertise, of his minute acquaintance with the Constitution of the Navy; of his razor-blade awareness of what was going on whether important or less important, of his affability that soothed or diminished occasions of disagreement or dispute; and above all of his unresting humanity, his concern for war victims or piracy victims or others defenceless against misfortune or want. If only it were possible, in so abbreviated an account, to follow up his endless provision for the Children of Christ's Hospital, the 'Blew Coate Boys: the Children shall have the full benefit of his Ma^ts allowance, without diminucon by fees or other charges: the sd Children shalbe by noe means comitted to uncertaine Masters or voyages: the Children should goe through the whole labour and practise of Navigacon.' Or again, the note of protection: 'Captains of all Sixth Rate Vessels must take an examination at Trinity House, since they are not allowed any master: and for the lives of those serving under them, ought to have their abilityes in Navigacon and Seamanship, inquired into and Certified.'

Abandoning these green fields reluctantly, we find that Charles, as much as he loves his ships, loves courage equally; to those who display it, 'his Ma^ty doth designe to show favour.'

'Captain Cuttance who faught soe well against pirates shall have comand of a good sayling Vessell of 12 or 14 guns.' Even above this might be cited 'the Medall and Chaine given to Captain Cranbrooke for his defence of the merchant ship *Pearle*: wherein having but 10 men and a Boye, in a fight with a Dutch pirate man'd with 56 men, he kill'd outright ye greater parte of ye Enemmy, and carried 13 prisoners into Lisbone.' In addition to Captain Cranbrooke's medal we are charmed to note that 'to each Man of the *Pearles* company, an order for 10£ a Man', and let us hope the 'Boye' was not forgotten. At the Council meeting of 14 November 1674 it seems that the King has lost sight of his promise 'to give to Captain Roach a Medall in reward for his extraordinary defence of his ship against two Dutch pirates': being reminded of this he is in genuine consternation, thanks the reminder heartily and arranges 'for Money for the Medall, to be supplyed at once.' On 11 September 1673 the King gives order 'to send away presently [immediately] some ships, to protect ye ffisheries and Colliery', but on the same date gives short shrift to a case either of cowardice or negligence: 'Captain Cotterill has not protected his convoy against pirates; he shalbe forthwith turned out of his Comand.' Knowing Charles, we are sure that the charges against Cotterill have been proved to the hilt. Charges of this sort, it may be noted, are extremely rare.

Quick mention should be made of the constant and desperate attempts to find some crack or cranny for 'ye great number of Seamen Criples, whoe are left out of any way of mainteyning them.' The Merchant Seamen having refused to have anything to do with them, a sort of stratagem is devised—whose feebleness and uncertainty are reflected in its first three words: 'Now and then, [they may have] a Cookes Place in his Mat^ys ships, as Vacancys fall.' The first trouble with this plan is, that such vacancies occur seldom; the second is that the injuries of candidates for the place are sometimes so frightful that reading of them still withers the heart, and the candidate himself is hardly equal to the humblest of kitchen jobs—let alone the hard working life of a cook. In full knowledge of this, the Council likewise orders a list classifying wounded seamen by geographical abode, so that 'Vacancys may be bestowed upon those, who live nearest to ye Hospitalls'.

On top of this is the lot, equally lamentable, of wounded officers: 'Captain John Pearce by ample Certificatts from Chirurgion John Knight, hath received such a Wound in his Head as hath brought upon him Convultion Fitts and weaknesse of sight.' Such cases get pensions as quickly as the King can give them out, always remembering that King and Council are equally impotent before contingencies requiring great sums of money. The deafening welter of cries and supplications from men and women both paralyse today's reader as it paralysed those who had to deal with it at first hand. The only comfort, even if a feeble one, is the nature of the help that was given when it was at all possible—its promptness and speed, without a wasted word or wasted moment. In the King's nature lay this immediacy of response to misery of every kind, as to bravery, kindness, ability—every facet that makes up the range of what we call goodness. And to its opposite—evil—his nature was by no means deficient in adequate response, when the occasion demanded it.

A CHANGE OF LAW

On 6 January 1675 was held a meeting of Council;* not only in full attendance, but having a special degree of interest through the presence of Sir Leoline Jenkins, Judge of the Admiralty Court. The reason for this comes up promptly: tomorrow (7 January) will be held the trial of an Ostend Caper (from now on called the Ostender) and her company, on the usual counts of piracy and murder. Yet this legal action, which may seem a usual routine, has been preceded by some unusual activity. Last

* Adm. 3–6 January 1675

night (5 January), at a special meeting of 'my Ld Chiefe Justice North, Mr Justice Wild, Mr Justice Ransford and three other officers plus the Sec'y of the Admiralty, Mr Samuel Pepys', the indictment of the pirates has gone through a preliminary examination and been heavily corrected. This is now submitted to the King: whether or not he suggested any of the corrections is not vouchsafed to us, but the chances are that he did. In any case, having approved it, Charles expresses the wish that 'some of the Lords of the Admiralty, my Lord Keeper if he could, my Lord Privy Seale, and as many more as would make a Quorum, should be present at the Tryall'.

This is most unusual and surprising, and at once imposes a sort of suspense. Will this revised indictment, which the King has just passed, stand up in action? Will the new form of law cover all aspects and contingencies, and will it go down well with the jury? Is it completely adequate, when practically applied?

Since in our source the indictment itself is never quoted, we can only follow passively in what tracks it has left. By 13 January the trial is over; two men, George Dickson alias Cusack, and Simon Harker, are to be executed. Accordingly Judge Sir Leoline 'presents their Lo^pps with two precedents' [very rare, this modern spelling] in 'an old form of warrants used in the time of ye Earle of Nothingham, for ye Executing of Persons then condemned to death for Piracy, by a Comission of Oyer and Terminer.' After some slight discussion—slight enough, evidently, to miss some important points—'their Lo^pps Resolved to keepe to ye same forme, with ye alteracons only of their Names as his Ma^tys Comission, instead of ye Lord High Admiral.'

At this point one of the neglected technicalities raises its ugly head. Beside the death sentences on two of the crew the Ostender itself has been penalized, and 'the Sherriff of London is laying claim, on behalfe of the City, to ye fine sett upon ye Ostender.' This claim finds everyone—the Lords, Sir Leoline, Mr Pepys himself—unprepared; after more discussion, somewhat uncertain this time, the Justice and Mr Pepys are ordered to confer with the Attorney-General and return with his opinion as soon as possible. In the meantime, 'ye Persons to be executed', and everyone else, must wait.

During the waiting pause however other aspects of the Ostender affair come up, and the Council—possibly exasperated with all the checks and delays—turns upon these with a vengeance. 'Resolved, that Captain Carverth be called to a Court Martiall, to answer his laying his head Saile to Maste, in submission to ye sd Ostender.' Having provided for Captain Carverth, the same meeting of Council continues striking out along the lines of similar charges; lack of respect to English ships, especially in home waters, is not to be endured for an instant.

At the Council meeting of 16 January, Judge Sir Leoline and Mr Pepys report on their search for expert opinion, a long session 'last night and this morning with my Ld Chiefe Justice North, for his advice touching ye forme of ye Warrant for ye Execucon of ye two Piratts: we have showne him Severall pracendents [sic] of Warrants on ye like occasion, signed by Admiralty officials.'

But now it is the Lord Chief Justice who rocks the boat; he has been thinking over his 'advice' and now—in his opinion—'the Warrant ought to runn in his Ma^{tys} Name'. He follows this up by repeating that the pirates should be executed not over the signature of 'Admiralty officials', but 'by his Ma^{tys} wish, and in his Name.' Therefore nothing is left for the Justice and Mr Pepys but to go back to Whitehall with this decision. The King is not in Council this morning but the four big guns present receive it, apparently, with perfect cordiality and willingness to change the warrant as indicated. Therefore 'by agreement of the Council, the Warrant is soe made out,' and can be applied as soon as it has the King's signature.

What happened next is minute in a historical sense, yet in its own way casts a fleeting light on event. The two men chiefly concerned in this transaction—Sir Leoline and Mr Pepys—set out for Whitehall instantly, undoubtedly relieved that the crisis was over, but also propelled by the steam of success. In their minds, in Pepys's especially, must have been the realization of another old piece of documentary lumber cast aside, another of those antiquated rulings—that clog the business of the courts —brought up to date. Side by side, in the warmest possible glow of achievement and self-approval, they walked the short distance; as the social inferior Mr Secretary Pepys probably carried the warrant, or if he had brought a clerk along, the clerk carried it, walking respectfully behind the two principals. In a few minutes they would have the royal signature, the King had not been at the last two council meetings but they knew he approved, of course he would sign on the instant . . .

At Whitehall, a check: his Majesty was out hunting. This news, with its prospect of delay, must have chilled them momentarily as much as anyone who, poised on an exciting verge, falls over it to the bottom. What the two men did then, we do not know; one guess is that they resolved to wait until the King had dined. If this is correct they probably renewed their forces with dinner at the Green Cloth (for distinguished visitors at court); the clerk or scribe, if any, was dispatched to pick up something where he could.

At last the great news percolated; his Majesty had returned and was just going to table. There only remains the question of how long they had to wait. Was Charles a thorough and lavish eater, did he rival in speed Queen Victoria, or did he come between? In view of his moderate temperament, probably the latter; not too little leisure for dignity and state, not too much for tediousness. At any rate, 'at his riseing from dinner', they nailed him on the instant. Immediately, having cast a knowledgeable eye on the changes, his signature changed the warrant into law, and now the pirates can swing in the odour of perfect legality.

XXI
Obstacles and Clearway

Any account of crime, including piracy, should progress neatly and consecutively in an agreed direction. First, the nailing of the criminal; then the trial; finally the sentence. No other order is possible, any lesser method should be regarded with the contempt it deserves.

Unfortunately, in spite of the most perfect agreement with this theory, any writer who draws his material from the sources quoted—the HCA Examinations and Acts—may be forced to concede the point little by little, and finally to abandon it. It is not the sheer volume of material which defeats him—for the more of this the better—but three other considerations, equally fatal to consecutive narrative: first, the lapses of time between testimony and trial, which may take place weeks, months or years after the witnesses have given evidence; second, the loss of relevant documents, and the loss is probably enormous beyond conjecture.

The third impediment, which has not been mentioned before, is as equally destructive of ordered narration as the other two, and this is a procedure of the Admiralty Court itself. Under its crushing programme of work and the growing necessity for short-cuts of some kind, it had become the habit of the Court— from what date it is impossible to say—to lump together a number of pirates *whose crimes were similar* and bring them all up for trial at once, regardless of different dates for the crimes committed and the different ships on which they originated. On this basis as many as five or six men might be tried together; the indictments seem not to name a greater number. Where murder was joined to piracy the warrant was restricted to two or three accused (seemingly) but we may assume that these were also eligible for trial—so to speak—by reason of proof by witnesses, or the pirates' own confession or partial confession.

From the despair and confusion which this system of multiple indictments creates in the reader, there is no escape. For example, we have seen that John Exton was what one might call a distinguished pirate, captain of various ships, guilty of at least one murder and object of governmental pursuit for over thirty years; yet again and again we will find Exton's name low down on the list of much humbler malefactors, and present along with other unknown offenders in any number of indictments or Juratores. If one had two or three lifetimes to do it in, it might be possible to read thousands of pages in order to isolate single names, tie them to the single or multiple crimes of which they were accused, and to trace the legal process from the examining Judge to the courtroom, and from the courtroom to Wapping or to freedom. Being possessor of only a normal span of existence one is defeated from the very beginning of the pursuit, though this sorrowful fact does not begin to dawn till the pursuer is trapped and immobilized in the very heart of the jungle. And in addition, to these three enemies of orderly narration is again the old, old impediment: the total absence of any word as to final decision in the vast majority of documents.

In the end, after all these attempts to skim the bottomless ocean with a teaspoon, what is left? The impressions are too jumbled and violent, the sources are too many: the never-ceasing clamour of voices lamenting, indignant or even foolish, in French, German, Spanish, Italian or Dutch, forever bleating in the Court with their tale of loss; the importunity of unimaginable distresses; witnesses in every language under the sun; the thousand thousand other cases that had nothing to do with piracy, the constant conflict (implied) between judges and juries determined to go their own way, the clerks' quill pens forever scratching on and on, the killing pressure of business that necessitated frequent Court sessions on Sunday. Yet with all this is left—curiously—a single impression growing stronger and stronger as one reads on and on—until it rears up majestically, blotting out lesser considerations, putting an end to contradictions and confusions, leaving as on a page one deep and clear imprint: the Admiralty Court in its tremendous labour of pursuing, with inviolate calm and for all men and women, that pitiless, troublesome and compassionate element called justice.

Index

Accidents at sea, 77–8, 99–100

Adey, John, captain of pirate vessel *Cordelia*, blackmailer, slave-trader, 97–8

Admiral, plundered merchant vessel, 56–9

Admiralty Court, The: Acts, 8, 83, 85, 126; buggery trials, 51–2; disappearance of records, 119, 126; documentary language, 108–10; Examinations, 6–8, *see also* Examinations; libel cases, 101–4; methods in piracy proceedings, 5–6, 126; origins, 5; poisoning cases, 105–7; preliminary recordings to sittings, 5–6; pressure of piracy trials, 47, 63, 126; trial of John Exton, 84–9

Andrewes, Tom, murdered on board *Hopewell*, 105

Andrewes, William, murdered on board *Hopewell*, 37

Angel, English merchant ship attacked by Spaniards, 93

'Annoying the Thames', 104

Armitage Dock, 104

Ascension, rescuer of the *Angel* and *Cherubim*, 93–5

Assize Courts, powers of, 13

Audley, William, tried for buggery, verdict *Ignoramus*, 51, 52

Baccaliere, Sebastian, owner of lading on the *Admiral*, 59–60

Bacon, Sir Francis, 16

Bail, granting of, 10, 11, 42

Barrenson, Tyfe, carpenter on the *Philip*, 59

Battles at sea, English v Scots, 95–6; English v Spanish, 93–5

Biddale, Robert, gentleman adventurer on board pirate vessel *Swan(n)*, 24

Billa Vera (True Bill), 32, 41, 44–5, 84

Black Horse, plundered merchant vessel, 47

Blessing, plundered merchant vessel, 49

Blevyn, Roland, pirate, executed, 9

Brewster, Thomas, and the stolen wax, 71–3

Brook, John, gentleman adventurer on board pirate vessel *Swan(n)*, 24

Brooke, Morgan, pirate, verdict *Ignoramus*, 42

Browne, Thomas, pirate, hanged, 33, 39

Bruen, John, captain of rival ship in Chimacha tragedy, 64–5

Buckingham, George, Duke of, Lord High Admiral, 113, 114, 116

Buggery, 51–2

Caesar, Sir Julius (1557–1636), Justice of Admiralty Court, 8, 16–17, 23, 24, 25, 42, 66

Calendar of State Papers Domestic, 119

Campion, Thomas, pirate, executed, 48

Campion, William, pirate, verdict *Ignoramus*, 47, 48

Cargoes, of pirated vessels: jewellery and gems, 30–3; mixed merchandise, 18, 20, 25, 28, 31–5, 34, 47, 48, 50; perishables, 110–12

Carle, Henry, captain of the *Philip*, 30, 59

Carnabie, witness in the Chimacha case, 63–4, 67

Cavard, Vincent, pirate, executed, 10

Chambers, Arthur, pirate, pardoned, 43

Charles I, King, 113, 116, 118, 119

Charles II, King, 119, 120, 124–5

Cherubim, English merchant ship attacked by Spaniards, 93–5

Chimacha, Spanish merchant, 63–7

Christmas, Peter, pirate, given bail, 42, 109

Christ's Hospital, 120–1

Cimba, plundered vessel carrying gems and jewellery, 31–2

Clark, Roger, survivor of storm, on *Rose Lyon*, 76–7

Classisq, Acquitan, pirate, executed, 36

Clerk(e), William, pirate, executed, 11, 36

Cobb, Robert, defendant in a raisin litigation, 110–11

Collins, Abraham, shanghaied by Exton, 87

Colthurst, master of the *True Love*, 101–104

Commerce, piracy effect on, 15

Commissions, Book of, 114–16

Communication, difficulties of notification abroad in piracy trials, 13–14

Confessions, 46–7

Corbus, Teye, pirate and murderer, verdict 'public beating', 54–5

Cordelia, pirate vessel, 97–8

Cornelison, Christopher, owner of the *St Mary*, 28–30

Cornelison, Christopher, pirate, 56–9

Cotterill, Captain, removed by Charles II from command, for cowardice against pirates, 121

Cottle, William, officer of the Admiralty Court, 73–5

Court of Admiralty, *see* Admiralty Court, The

Coventry, Sir Thomas, 116, 120

Cox, Daniell, pirate, executed, 37, 38

Cranbrooke, Captain, rewarded for courage, by Charles II, with medal and chain, 121

Crippled seamen, care of, 121

Croker, captain of the *Reprisal*, 30, 95–6

Cromer, John, merchant and co-owner of the *Mary*, 19–20, 23, 24

Crompton, Sir Thomas, Judge in Admiralty Court, 68–71

Crump, Titus, witness to storm-death of Captain Thomas Mourne, 77–8

Cumberland, Earl of, 25

Cumberland, Simon, poisoned by Hugh Davies on board the *Samuel and Henry*, 105

Curtis, William, pirate, given bail, later hanged, 42, 46

Custer, John, pirate, hanged, 33, 39

Cuttance, Captain, rewarded by Charles II for courage against pirates, 121

Dales, Martyn, pilot of the *Mary*, 22–3

Darling, vessel damaged in the Thames, 99–100

Davies, Hugh, killer of John Harmon and poisoner of Simon Cumberland on the *Samuel and Henry*, 105–6

Death sentence on pirates, 11–13; *see also* Executions; Southwark; Wapping

Deveninge, William, pirate, executed, 32

Dickson, George (alias Cusack), pirate on the *Ostender*, executed, 123–5

Dier, a porter in the case of the stolen wax, 71–3

Disease at sea, 79–82

Disloyalty to King on board ship, 118

Dolphin, pirate vessel, 37

Drake, Sir Francis, involvement in piracy, 60, 83

Dress, mode of merchants and seamen in seventeenth century, 21

Dyckman, William, witness in case of the stolen glove, 102–3

Effingham, Charles, Earl of, 40

Elizabeth I, Queen, 16, 47; piracy under, 7, 36, 37, 38, 84

Escott, George, resisting Warrant for arrest, 73–5

Examinations in Admiralty Court cases, 6–8, 9, 10, 11, 12, 16, 83, 85, 100, 126; Chimacha tragedy, 63–7; contracts for ship repairs, 100; Christopherus Cornelison of the *St Mary*, 28–30; John Cromer of the *Mary*, 19–25; disloyalty to King, 118–19; followed by Interrogatory, 7–8; grafitti on documents, 109–10; method of conducting, 7; Antonio de Morera of the *St Anthony*, 25–7; Richard Norgrave of the *Bonaventure*, 68–71; John Seline of the *Trinity*, 17–19; Thomas Waighte for plundering the *Cimba*, 31–2; Elizabeth Wilkinson in the case of the stolen glove, 102–4

Executioners, 48

Executions: for murder, 36–40, 45, 46, 47, 97, 123; *Ostender* case, 123; for piracy, 11–12, 33, 123; *see also* Southwark; Wapping

Exton, John, pirate and merchant, 83–9;

escape from prison, 84; murder trial, 38, 127; subsequent trials, 83–9

Fenner, William, pirate, freed, 44
ffaster, George, pirate, executed for murder, 39
ffaverus (Faveras), Jaques, murdered by pirates, 37, 38, 45, 84
ffisher, Richard, pirate, pardoned, 43
fflaute, John, witness in Chimacha tragedy, 65–6
ffold, Edward, killer of Tom Andrewes on *Hopewell*, poisoner of Mr Thompson on *Mistress*, 105, 106
ffurnace, Andrewe, murdered mariner, 37
ffurnace, Audrey, owner of *Susan*, 39
Figs as cargo, 111–12
Flower of Luce, plundered merchant vessel, 45
Foreign nationals: on piracy charges, 13; ships plundered by English, 13, 32, 33, 34, 36, 46, 48, 56–60, 93–4
Fuggers, 13

Gallows, Southwark, 11; Wapping, 11, 12; *see also* Executions
Gamaliell, vessel damaged in the Thames, 99–100
Gascon, Norman, pirate, executed, 36
George, plundered vessel, 34
Ghoste, vessel granted Letter of Reprisal, 114
Gift of God, vessel granted Letter of Reprisal, 113
Gilbert, Sir John, owner of *Reprisal*, 30; piracy proceeds involvement, 60
Green Dragon, pirate vessel, captained by John Exton, 87
Greenlese, Richard, pirate, sentenced *Peine Forte et Dure*, 64–5
Grewe, Jo., merchant, 37
Gryffyn, Johannes, pirate, executed, 11, 36
Guerin, John, victim of John Exton's piracies, 88; witness in Exton trial, 38

Hall, Edward, pirate, executed, 44–5
Harker, Simon, pirate of the *Ostender*, executed, 123–5
Harmon, John, murdered by Hugh

Davies on board the *Samuel and Henry*, 106
Harper, John, pirate, executed, 32
Harris, Richard, pirate, 34
Harrison, William, defendant in a raisin litigation, 110–11
Harrod, Robertus de Rye, pirate, hanged, 45
Harvy, William, sentenced *Peine Forte et Dure*, 53–4
Hatten, Sir Christopher, 31
Haydon, Richard, pirate, executed for murder, 39
Henry, Prince, 41
Hewitt, Robert, tried for buggery, verdict *Ignoramus*, 51–2
Hicks, Robert, pirate, executed, 10
High Court of Admiralty (HCA), *see* Admiralty Court, The
Hiscock, Mr, owner of the *Darling*, 99–100
Homosexuality, *see* Buggery
Hopewell, merchant vessel, 37, 42; murder on, 37, 42, 105; plundering of, 83–4
Howard, Lord Admiral Charles, 113, 116
Hugan, Eyvan, pilot of *Trinity*, 18–19
Humfrey, George, pirate, executed for murder, 39

Ignoramus ('Don't know'), verdict leading to acquital, 10, 42–3, 84
Indictments, multiple, 126–7
Informers, 118–19; rewards, 118
Inner Temple, 16
Inquiratur, 15–16, 81, 83, 84; of John Exton, 83–9, 127
Interpreters, use of in Admiralty Court, 6, 17, 25, 27, 56, 68, 95
Interrogatory, 7, 16, 58; of John Poindexter, 92; in raisin case, 111; of Elizabeth Wilkinson, 101–4

Jacob, see St Jacob
Jackson, Arthur, tried for buggery, verdict *Ignoramus*, 51
Jaques de Octe, plundered vessel, 36
James I, King, 5, 15, 37, 42, 47
Jenkins, Sir Leoline, Judge of the Admiralty Court, 122, 123, 124
Jennings, John, pirate, given bail, later hanged, 42, 46

Jewellery, its place in seventeenth century fashion, 30–1

Johnson, owner of the *St John*, 63

Jonas, pirate vessel, 36

Jones, Robert, pirate, condemned and pardoned for murder, 37, 42

Jones, William, pirate, hanged, 33, 39

Juratores, 8–9, 127

Jurors, disagreements among, 39, 46, 127; lists of, 8

Justices of Admiralty Court, 6–8, 16

Keeler, Alice, woman victim of *Peine Forte de Dure*, 55

Keeler, Thomas, hanged for murder, 55

Kerke, Captain Lewis, receiver of a Letter of Reprisal, 114

Kettelly, Charles, pirate, pardoned, 41

Kirkman, captain of the *Ascension*, 94–5

Kitchin, Robert, receiver of Letter of Reprisal, 113

Language, documentary of Admiralty Court in sixteenth–seventeenth centuries, 108–10

Lashbrooke, Lewis, attorney, 73–5

Latin, Juratores written in, 8–9, 108–9; use of in Admiralty Court documents, 6, 108

Lawrence, Thomas, pirate, executed for murder, 37

Leash, Abigail, merchant, 34

Letters of Reprisal, 25, 29, 113–17; ships granted, 113, 114, 116; wording of, 114–16

Lewis, Robertus, pirate, executed, 11, 36

Libel case, 103

London, Sheriff of, 123

Longe, John, pirate, executed for murder, 37, 38

Lord High Admiral, 17, 18

Magdalen, plundered merchant vessel, 48

Manning, pirate ship-owner and accomplice of John Exton, 86–8

Marden, Sir Henry, Judge High Court of Admiralty, 113–14

Marten, Henrico, Dr of Law, murdered by female pirate Elizabeth Patrickson, 49, 50

Martin, Justice Henry, 34

Martyn, John, captain of pirate vessel *Swan(n)*, 20–1, 23

Marshalsea (prison), 36, 40, 47, 51, 84, 88

Mary, plundered vessel, 19–25

Mary, Queen, 16

Mary, vessel, situ of Audley's buggery, 31

Merchant seamen, 121

Mermaid, merchant vessel, 37, 38; plundering of, 84

Midleton, gentleman adventurer on pirate vessel *Swan(n)*, 20, 23–4

Mollett, Edward, pirate, executed for murder, 39

Moore, John, captain of the *St John*, 63–6

Morera, Antonio de, master of the *St Anthony*, 25–7

Morocco, slave trade, 5, 15

Motham, James, master of the *Bonaventure*, 68–71

Mourne, Thomas, captain of the *Emily*, drowned at sea, 77–8

Moxiner, Clement, pilot of the *St Anthony*, 27

Murder with piracy, 36–40, 45, 46, 47, 97, 123

Names (of persons), amusing examples of English and Dutch sixteenth–seventeenth centuries, 109

Navy, 118–21

Newgate gaol, 49

Newport, John, lieutenant of pirate vessel *Swan(n)*, 21–2

Norgrave, Richard, merchant, 68–71

Norris, John, resisting of Warrant arrest, 73–5

North, Lord Chief Justice, 123, 124

Nottingham, Lord Charles, Earl of, 53, 54, 123

Orders, in Admiralty Court trials, 9

Ostender, pirate vessel, charges against leading to a change in law, 122–5

Pansfoote, Giles, receiver of pirate loot, 48–9

Parchment, use of in Admiralty Court documents, 8

Patrickson, Elizabeth, woman pirate, tortured, fate unknown, 49–50

Paule, Thomas, pirate, hanged, 33, 39

Pearl, plundered vessel, 34, 121

Peine Forte et Dure, 10, 53–5; description of, 54

Pemberton, John, suer in raisin litigation, 110–11

Pensions, 122

Pepys, Samuel, 116, 120, 123, 124

Peterson, Reiner, purser on the *St Mary*, 30

Phelips, Robert, pirate, of the *Rebecca*, 34

Philip, pirate vessel, 28–30, 56–9

Piracy: bloodless, 15; effect on commerce, 15, 119; in Elizabeth I's reign, 7, 36, 37, 38, 84; exploits of the *Philip*, 28–30, 56–9; instructed and condoned by Royal approval, *see* Letters of Reprisal; in James I's reign, 5, 15, 37, 42, 47; and murder, 36–40, 45, 46, 47, 97, 123; and poisoning, 105–7; raids on towns and villages, 5

Pirates: condemned to death, 11–13, 33, 39, 40, 45, 46, 47, 97; *see also* individual cases

Plague devastation on the *St Jacob*, 79–81; survivors rescued by English ships, 80–1

Poindexter, John, hijacker and pirate, 90–2

Poisoning on board ship, 105–7

Pope, John, pirate, imprisonment, 46

Pope, William, pilot, murdered, 39

Pope, William, pirate, imprisonment, 47

Powell, Rowland, gentleman adventurer on pirate vessel *Swan(n)*, 24

Precepts in Admiralty Court trials, 9, 10, 12

Presentments in Admiralty Court trials, 9, 12, 49, 50

Raisins, litigation over, 110–11

Raleigh, Sir Walter, involved in piracy, 31, 83

Ransford, Mr Justice, 123

Rawlyns, William, captain of the hijacked *Golden Calf*, 91

Rebecca, pirate vessel, 34

Receivers of pirated loot, 48–9

Reprisal, pirate vessel, 30, 95–6

Richardson, William, accomplice in Exton's escape, 84

Roach, Captain, rewarded with medal by Charles II for courage against piracy, 121

Robinson, Hugo, pirate, verdict *Ignoramus*, 43

Rombles, a pirate, 18

Rose Lyon, withstands tempestuous storm, 76–7

Royal Exchange, 14

Royall Mary, vessel, situ of Hewitt's buggery, 51–2

Sackeld, a pirate, 18

St Anthony, plundered vessel, 25–7

St Jacob, ravaged by a plague, 79–81

St John, merchant ship involved in Chimacha tragedy, 63–7

St Mary, plundered vessel, 28–30, 56–9

St Vincent, Admiral Earl, 51, 77

Sallowes, John, pirate, executed, 45

Samuel and Henry, scene of murder of Simon Cumberland and John Harmon, 106

Scaddon, Josias, accomplice of Exton, 86–7

Scots ships in combat with English, 95–96

Scurvy, 79

Scottle, Gerrard, pirate, hanged, 47

Sea, perils of, 76–82

Seale, Thomas, pirate, executed, 36

Sefton gallows, 39, 44

Seline, John, captain of the *Trinity*, 17–19

Serena, plundered merchant vessel, 37, 38, 84

Sezar, *see* Caesar, Sir Julius

Sherlock, Richard, pirate, executed, 47–48

Ship money, 118

Ships: dimensions of types plundered, 15; names of, grotesque examples, 109; *see also under names*

Sickness at sea, 79–82

Skulduggery in shipping deals, 68–75

Slave trade, 5, 15, 29

Southwark, 44; executions at, 11, 36, 40, 46, 47, 97; piracy trials at, 14, 40

Spaniards: reprisals against, 113–14; sea battles with, 93–5

Speedwell, plundering and murder on, 45

Stadding, Richard, accomplice of Exton, 86

Stafford, Richard, witness against Exton, 87–8

Steelyard, 13–14, 21

Strangulation as punishment, 39, 46

Stych, a pirate, 34

Surety, situ of Audley's buggery, 51

Susan, Andrewe ffurnace and Audrey ffurnace murdered on board, 37, 39

Suspensus erat, 41–50

Swan(n), pirate vessel, 20–5

Sweepstake, pirate vessel, 36

Talbot, pirate vessel, 37, 84

Taylor, Francis, defendant in raisin litigation, 110–11

Thames river, contamination of, 104

Thomasine, pirate vessel, 37, 84

Thompson, victim of poisoning on board *Mistress*, 105

Tompkins, Thomas, pirate, condemned but died in prison, 48

Torture, 49, 50

Trevor, Richard, pirate, imprisonment, 46

Trials, in Admiralty Court, 5–13, 36–40; advertisement of, 13–14

Trinity House, 121

Trinity, plundered merchant vessel, 17–18

True Love, vessel in case of the stolen glove, 101–4

Typhus, 79

Vaack, Nicholas, pirate, 34, 35

Vaults, hangings in, 45–6

Vice-Admiral, plundered merchant vessel, 56–9

Vogle, Otto, quasi-owner of the *St Mary*, 28

Waighte, Thomas, pirate, plunderer of the *Cimba* gems cargo, 31

Walpole, John, an informer, 118

Wapping, 44, 127; executions at, 11, 12, 33, 39, 45, 46, 47, 97; ship gossip at, 101–4

Ward, Philip, sentenced *Peine Forte et Dure*, 53

Warrants in Admiraltly Court trials, 9–10, 12, 35, 38, 83; change in law regarding signature to, 124; for execution, scarcity of, 11–12; legalizing of, 125; serving of, 73–4

Weston, Sarah, merchant, 34

Wild, Mr Justice, 128

Wilkinson, Elizabeth, witness in case of stolen glove, 102–4

Wine as cargo, 111–12

Woodwarde, John, witness in raisin litigation, 111

WAPP